# HEADLINE SERIES

No. 322        FOREIGN POLICY ASSOCIATION        Summer 2001

# PAKISTAN
## FLAWED NOT FAILED STATE

Cover Design: Agnes Kostro                                    $5.95

Cover Photo: ©Christine Osborne/CORBIS. A Pakistani tilework.

## The Author

Dennis Kux is a retired State Department South Asia specialist and the author of *The United States and Pakistan, 1947–2000: Disenchanted Allies*, just published by the Wilson Center and Johns Hopkins University presses. A companion history, *India and the United States, 1941–1991: Estranged Democracies*, was first printed in 1993. The author, who has just returned from India and Pakistan, is currently a Senior Scholar at the Woodrow Wilson Center in Washington, D.C.

## The Foreign Policy Association

The Foreign Policy Association is a private, nonprofit, nonpartisan educational organization. Its purpose is to stimulate wider interest and more effective participation in, and greater understanding of, world affairs among American citizens. Among its activities is the continuous publication, dating from 1935, of the HEADLINE SERIES. The author is responsible for factual accuracy and for the views expressed. FPA itself takes no position on issues of U.S. foreign policy.

HEADLINE SERIES (ISSN 0017-8780) is published four times a year, Spring, Summer, Fall and Winter, by the Foreign Policy Association, Inc., 470 Park Avenue So., New York, NY 10016. Chairman, Dave Williams; President, Noel V. Lateef; Editor in Chief, Karen M. Rohan; Managing Editor, Ann R. Monjo; Associate Editors, Nicholas Y. Barratt and Agnes Kostro; Editorial Assistant, Anna Melman. Subscription rates, $20.00 for 4 issues; $35.00 for 8 issues; $50.00 for 12 issues. Single copy price $5.95; double issue $11.25; special issue $10.95. Discount 25% on 10 to 99 copies; 30% on 100 to 499; 35% on 500 and over. Payment must accompany all orders. Postage and handling: $2.50 for first copy; $.50 each additional copy. Second-class postage paid at New York, NY, and additional mailing offices. POSTMASTER: Send address changes to HEADLINE SERIES, Foreign Policy Association, 470 Park Avenue So., New York, NY 10016. Copyright 2001 by Foreign Policy Association, Inc. Design by Agnes Kostro. Printed at Science Press, Ephrata, Pennsylvania. Published Summer 2001.

Library of Congress Control Number: 2001091750
ISBN 0-87124-198-6

# Introduction

I N "PAKISTAN: Flawed Not Failed State," Dennis Kux provides an informative, and sometimes provocative, political/economic history of Pakistan from its inception in 1947 to the present. Equally he offers a cogent overview of U.S.-Pakistan relations during this often turbulent period.

While having more than its share of challenges and troubles, as Kux concludes, Pakistan does not fit the "failed state" syndrome, riven by civil wars, unable to defend its borders and incapable of dealing with the outside world. Scholar-economist Shahid Javed Burki's characterization of Pakistan

---

*by John C. Monjo*

John C. Monjo served as U.S. ambassador to Pakistan from 1992 to 1995. A Wharton School graduate and longtime East Asia specialist, Monjo was ambassador to Malaysia, 1987–89, and to Indonesia, 1989–92.

as "A Nation in the Making" may be nearer the mark.

Many Americans, including those who follow foreign affairs closely, have only a limited knowledge of Pakistan and the frequently bumpy relationship it has enjoyed (or endured) with the United States. There are many reasons why Pakistan is important to the United States and to the world at large. A medium-sized country of about 150 million ( a number which will double in a generation if the present birthrate continues), Pakistan holds a strategic place geographically, with such varied neighbors as India, China, Afghanistan and Iran. Despite intense pressure from extremist Islamic elements, both domestic and foreign, and intermittent Sunni-Shia disputes internally, Pakistan has so far remained moderate religiously, as evidenced in national elections where extremist parties obtain only a negligible percentage of the vote. Americans of Pakistani descent, plus legal and illegal immigrants to the United States, total at least 300,000, with the number growing steadily. While their political clout is still limited, they are hard working and prosperous, and increasingly aware that they should be active on the political scene.

On a less positive note, Pakistan's support for the extremist Taliban regime in Afghanistan causes the United States, and much of the world, considerable concern. Finally, Pakistan's difficult relations with its mammoth neighbor to the east, India, do not bode well for the stability of the region. Since 1998, with both of these countries declared nuclear-weapons states, their long border, including disputed Kashmir, has become one of the most troubling flash points in the world.

Despite these factors, there has been, particularly pre-1998, a sentiment among many in the U.S. body politic that Washington could deal with Pakistan pretty much as it chose, with few downsides to whatever stance it adopted. As one congressman, a well-wisher of Pakistan, put it privately, "They need us a lot more than we need them." Thus, if the United States wanted Pakistan's assistance, as during the Afghan war to expel the Soviets, it could count on it, while offering substantial amounts of economic and military aid. Conversely, if the United States were unhappy with Pakistan's policies or behavior, as in the case of its development of a nuclear-weapons capability, it could cool relations and withhold aid with little fear of retaliation.

Seemingly lost in this equation was a realization that, even when relations were at a low ebb, things could be a lot worse from the U.S. point of view if the Pakistan government adopted different policies. For example, leading figures from both American political parties, plus top military officers, have commented that extremely anti-American regimes had often sought Pakistan's cooperation in developing advanced military weapons, offering important financial compensation. Pakistan, they added, declined to accept these offers.

A bilateral relationship is inevitably viewed differently by the leaders and citizens of the two countries involved. In the case of the United States and Pakistan, the gap may be one of the largest existing between basically friendly countries.

Successive U.S. Administrations have been disappointed that a system of democratically elected governments has not prevailed in Pakistan, despite the massive development assistance Washington has offered on several occasions. Perhaps in part because of this, the United States has tended to reward or punish Pakistan for its policies and actions, e.g., its relations with the U.S.S.R., China and India, its involvement in the Afghan war, and most recently its development of a nuclear-weapons capability.

Currently Washington is deeply concerned over the three issues noted by Kux: Pakistan's support for the Kashmir insurgency, its backing of the Taliban in Afghanistan and its nuclear policies. Also, although the United States must be careful about interfering in the domestic affairs of a friendly country, it is anxious about the timing and smoothness of Pakistan's return to a democratically elected government.

Pakistan, for its part, would like to see among U.S. priorities some form of involvement in a resolution of Indo-Pakistan differences. Optimally, Islamabad would like Washington to offer mediation, but informed Pakistanis realize that without India's concurrence (most unlikely) this is probably a nonstarter.

Many Pakistanis, including large numbers of the elite who enroll their children in prestigious U.S. universities, complain that the United States is an inconsistent (some say faithless) friend. For example, Washington has viewed Pakistan's consistently friendly relations with China through the prism of U.S. China policy, without sufficient appreciation of Pakistan's need to protect its own interests. Thus at one point the United States punished Pakistan for its close ties to Beijing, while a few years later Washington used Pakistan as a jumping-off point to smuggle the U.S. secretary of state into China to begin negotiations leading to normalization of relations with that country.

Again, Pakistanis note that when they worked with the

United States to push the Soviets out of Afghanistan, Washington promised assistance in dealing with the inevitable negative side effects of the conflict. As a result of the Afghan war, areas of Pakistan suffer from the violence and lawlessness of the "Kalashnikov culture," all of the country endures a drug culture that was virtually nonexistent before the war, large numbers of poor Afghan refugees remain in Pakistan, and Balochistan has been deforested by refugees cutting down the trees. The United States, citing Pressler restrictions which required cutting off aid when Pakistan was judged to have a nuclear capability, ended all assistance, leaving Pakistan to deal with the aftermath of the war on its own.

Events reflecting well on Pakistan appear to Islamabad to obtain only passing attention in the United States. The Pakistan government, in the second half of the 1990s, showed increased willingness to assist U.S. investigations into terrorist acts: suspected World Trade Center bomber Ramzi Ahmed Yousef and Mir Aimal Kasi, accused of killing two Central Intelligence Agency employees, were both extradited. These actions were not popular with a large segment of the Pakistani populace and required considerable courage on the part of the authorities. In part as a sign of friendship, Pakistan joined the UN force in Somalia at the direct request of President George H.W. Bush; the Pakistanis then stayed on after the United States withdrew, following a direct appeal from President Bill Clinton.

The past is the past, and despite whatever errors there may have been on either or both sides, the U.S.-Pakistan relationship remains fundamentally strong. As a friend of Pakistan, and in its own enlightened interest, the United States should seek ways to strengthen bilateral ties, based on shared political and economic values and interests, not merely on cooperation in dealing with an individual event such as the Soviet occupation of Afghanistan.

With Gen. Pervez Musharraf's pledge to hold elections in late 2002, Washington has a year to offer appropriate assistance to help ensure that the results are credible and that a duly elected government is in place. Additionally, the United States should explore ways, some of which may require congressional action, to offer some degree of cooperation in the economic and social areas.

Pakistan and U.S.- Pakistan relations are too important for benign neglect.

April 2001
Washington, D.C.

# Foreword

ON AUGUST 7, 1947, the tall, gaunt figure of 70-year-old Muhammad Ali Jinnah, the leader of India's Muslims, stepped onto the tarmac at Pakistan's Karachi airport after flying from New Delhi, India, to take charge of a new nation for whose birth he was largely responsible. A week later, on August 14, 1947, Lord Louis Mountbatten, the last viceroy of British India, joined Jinnah to proclaim the independence of Pakistan. Cheering crowds in Karachi, then the capital, welcomed the new country with great enthusiasm and satisfaction.

The fledgling nation of 75 million people faced enormous challenges, not the least of which was its unusual geographic makeup—the western and eastern parts of Pakistan were separated by over a thousand miles of Indian territory. The west, which stretched northward along the arid Indus River valley from the Arabian Sea to the lofty Himalayan mountains, comprised the Punjab, Sindh, the Northwest Frontier Province (NWFP) and Balochistan. The eastern wing, then called East

Bengal and later East Pakistan, was carved out of Muslim majority areas of Bengal and Assam provinces. In contrast to the dry west, the east comprised the lush and moist delta of the Ganges and Brahmaputra rivers. There was little that the two parts of Pakistan shared other than the bond of Islam and their dislike of India. They did not even have a common language. Urdu provided a lingua franca for the west; the easterners spoke Bengali.

The creation of Pakistan marked the successful culmination of a decade-long struggle by Jinnah and his colleagues in the Muslim League, the major political voice for India's 100 million Muslims. A quarter of India's population, the Muslim minority feared that it would be unfairly treated by the Hindus after the British left. In March 1940, the Muslim League called for splitting British India into two independent states—one with a Hindu majority to remain as India and the other with a Muslim majority, to be called Pakistan. Although at first the two-nation theory was not taken too seriously, when the Muslim League swept the Muslim seats in 1945–46 elections for an Indian constituent assembly, the question of creating Pakistan became the burning issue in negotiations about India's future. Neither the British nor the largely Hindu Indian National Congress (INC) party wanted to accept partition, but they reluctantly agreed after negotiations reached an irreconcilable impasse and after unprecedented Hindu-Muslim communal violence scarred India during 1946 and 1947.

Fifty-four years after independence, the bright promise on which Pakistan was founded has vanished, following a disappointing and often sad first half century. The east wing, dissatisfied with its treatment by the west, became a separate country, Bangladesh, after the 1971 India-Pakistan war. Since then, a shrunken Pakistan has failed to achieve political stability, sustained economic growth, or a clear sense of national identity. In 1986, scholar-economist Shahid Javed Burki subtitled his study of Pakistan *A Nation in the Making*. Fifteen years later, it remains a nation in the making.

Indeed, in recent years, Pakistan's future has become a

source of worry in Washington and other major world capitals. There is anxiety that having backed the fundamentalist Taliban in Afghanistan and *jihad* or "holy war" against India in Kashmir, Pakistan itself may be drifting toward Islamic fundamentalism. There is further concern that with India and Pakistan declared nuclear-weapons states, their festering tensions over Kashmir may slip out of control and risk the nightmare scenario of the world's first use of nuclear weapons since the World War II bombings of the Japanese cities of Hiroshima and Nagasaki.

The author traces political, economic and social developments in Pakistan and the evolution of its foreign and security policies over the past half century to help the reader understand how a nation that was America's "most allied ally in Asia" in the 1950s, and its indispensable partner against the Soviet occupation of Afghanistan during the 1980s, has fallen on such troubled and dangerous times.

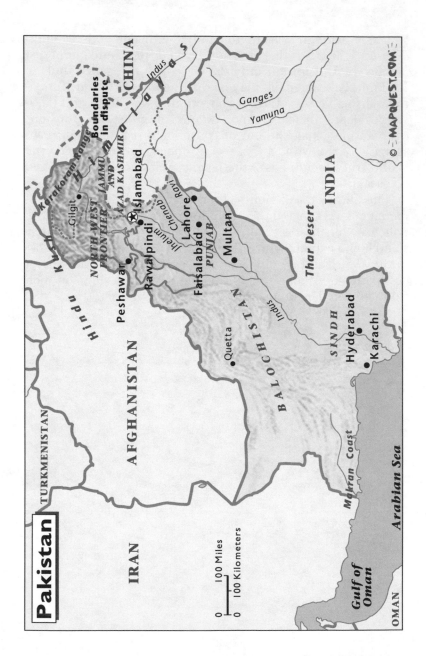

# 1

# Chronic Political Instability

WHEN PAKISTAN gained independence, it faced the daunting task of establishing a new central government from scratch, of feeding and sheltering millions of Muslim refugees who had fled their homes in India, and of addressing a host of thorny administrative problems over the division of the physical and financial assets of British India. Then, just 13 months later, in September 1948, Jinnah, the nation's founding father and towering political leader, died of tuberculosis. Three years later, Pakistan suffered a second heavy loss when his successor, Prime Minister Liaqat Ali Khan, was assassinated. The disappearance of the two most popular and capable public figures so soon after Pakistan's birth proved a devastating political blow. To make matters worse, within months of independence, war broke out with India over the princely state of Jammu and Kashmir, setting the stage for chronic tension and three wars with Pakistan's larger neighbor.

In Karachi, the constituent assembly, whose members were chosen in British India's 1945–46 elections, struggled in vain for nearly a decade to adopt a constitution. The major differences were over the role of Islam and the division of power between the provinces and the central government. Not until March 1956 were the legislators able to agree on a constitution that established a largely secular and centralized state. Seats in the national assembly were divided equally between the more populous East Pakistan and the physically larger west, where the four provinces were combined into the single administrative unit called West Pakistan.

The Muslim League lacked goals beyond creating Pakistan and began to unravel after achieving this. A disparate conglomeration of "feudal" landlords from the Punjab, squabbling politicians from East Bengal, conservative Muslim clerics, and refugees from India, the Muslim League suffered a crushing defeat in 1954 provincial assembly elections in East Bengal. Running on a platform of Bengali grievances against the central government in Karachi, the opposition United Front swept 223 assembly seats compared to a meager 10 for the Muslim League.

By the mid-1950s, the Muslim League was no longer an effective national political organization. The essence of political power had passed into the hands of the senior civil service and military leadership, which mainly came from West Pakistan. Skeptical that the country with a largely illiterate and predominantly peasant population was ready for democracy, many in the ruling elite believed a quasi-authoritarian government not unlike the British Raj (rule) would be better for Pakistan. In foreign policy, the new rulers in Karachi pressed hard and ultimately successfully to make Pakistan a military ally of the United States. While strongly anti-Communist, Liaqat and other political leaders had been reluctant to tie their country to the West unless Pakistan received a firm security guarantee against an attack by India, something that Washington was unwilling to provide.

Elections under the 1956 constitution, scheduled for 1958 but postponed until 1959, never took place. Widespread political unrest in both wings culminated in September 1958 with the death of Shahid Ali, the deputy speaker of the East Pakistan provincial assembly, after he was hit on the head by an

14

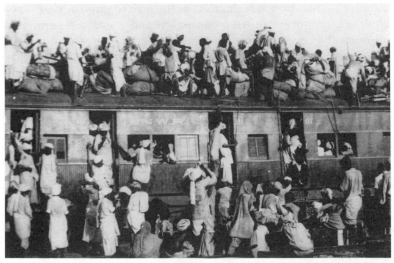

AP/Wide World Photos

**Hundreds of Muslims crowd a train leaving New Delhi for Pakistan following Britain's creation of two independent states, India and Pakistan, from its Indian Empire.**

inkwell during a melee in the assembly chambers in Dhaka. This proved the last straw for President Iskander Mirza, a former army officer and civil servant in British India, and Gen. Muhammad Ayub Khan, the army commander in chief. The pair seized power on October 7, 1958, abrogated the 1956 constitution and imposed martial law. Three weeks later, Ayub sent Mirza off into exile in Britain and became Pakistan's first military dictator, combining the functions of chief martial law administrator, president and commander in chief of the army.

### *Military Rule: From 1958 to 1969*

Ayub largely kept the soldiers in the barracks and ruled through the civil service, acting much like a viceroy in British India. He adopted a number of reforms, including the modern-

15

ization of education, a reduction in the size of large agricultural holdings, an anticorruption campaign and a greater emphasis on market economic forces. He also decided to build a new capital, Islamabad, in the foothills of the Himalayas, 800 miles north of Karachi. Even though Ayub controlled the press and initially sidelined political parties and politicians, Pakistanis felt satisfied that their country was starting to tackle the tasks of nation building.

During the first years of Ayub's effective if not very democratic rule, Pakistan seemed to be progressing in a promising manner. In 1962, martial law was lifted and a new constitution was imposed that provided for a strong president and a weak national legislature. Some 80,000 local counselors or "basic democrats," chosen by universal suffrage, elected the president and members of the national assembly. Under this indirect system, Ayub won only an unimpressive victory over Fatima Jinnah, the sister of Pakistan's founder, in 1965 elections, despite the active support of the administrative apparatus. Respected but not loved as a leader, Pakistan's president lacked a politician's touch in dealing with the public.

Ayub might have succeeded, nonetheless, in institutionalizing his political system had he not stumbled into war with India in September 1965 in an effort to gain Kashmir by force. Although the conflict was a draw militarily, India won by not losing. The president's prestige suffered badly. East Pakistan's defenselessness during the conflict aggravated the province's grievances against the west, fueling Bengali demands for far greater provincial autonomy. West Pakistanis, who were misled by government propaganda to believe that India had lost the war, were dismayed by Ayub's failure to achieve any gains from the fighting.

Politically wounded by the fallout of the war, which included the loss of U.S. military assistance, and physically weakened by illness, the once confident Ayub faltered when the opposition took to the streets in 1968. Leading the charge was former foreign minister Zulfikar Ali Bhutto, who sharply criticized the peace agreement that Ayub had reached with India under Soviet mediation at Tashkent, U.S.S.R., in January 1966. Bhutto advocated a more nationalist, anti-American, pro-China foreign policy and urged a shift from free-market to socialist economic policies. Unable to calm the disorders, a sad Ayub Khan stepped down in March 1969, handing over power to Army Chief Gen. Agha Muhammad Yahya Khan.

## New Military Dictator: From 1969 to 1971

Pakistan's second military dictator promptly imposed martial law and abrogated Ayub's 1962 constitution. Although Yahya Khan saw himself as a transitional figure preparing the country for democratic elections, he took several important political steps. He broke up the single administrative unit in the west and restored the four provincial governments. He increased development spending in the east and also ended parity between the wings for the proposed 1970 national elections. Yahya's decision to allot seats on the basis of population meant that the more populous East Pakistan would have a majority in the national assembly. Regrettably, Yahya did not tackle the thorniest issue—how to divide power between East Pakistan and the central government. Two years later, the inability of the elected leaders to solve this problem led to Pakistan's breakup.

In December 1970, when Pakistanis voted in their first-ever democratic national election, the results were a stunning surprise. In the east, the pro-autonomy Awami League, led by Sheikh Mujibur Rahman, had been expected to win easily, but not to sweep 160 of 162 seats and thereby gain an absolute majority in the national assembly. In the four western provinces, Zulfikar Ali Bhutto's new Pakistan People's Party (PPP) obtained a clear majority of seats, upsetting the traditional parties with his populist slogan of "Bread, Clothing and Shelter." The fact that the Awami League won no seats in the west and the PPP none in the east underscored the polarization of Pakistani politics.

After Yahya, Bhutto and Mujibur Rahman failed to settle the burning question of provincial autonomy, Yahya and the military decided to resolve the issue by force rather than accept a weak central government or a peaceful split between the two parts of the country. In March 1971, the president outlawed the Awami League, arrested Mujibur Rahman and ordered his soldiers, almost entirely from West Pakistan, to crush the East Pakistanis. As millions of refugees fled to India, the army initially gained the upper hand. But with covert support from New Delhi, a guerrilla movement developed and gradually rendered the province ungovernable.

In November–December 1971, the Indian army moved into East Pakistan to start the third Indo-Pakistan war. The outnumbered Pakistan army fought as well as it could, but after two weeks it surrendered and East Pakistan became the independent state of Bangladesh. Yahya resigned in disgrace, turning over control of West Pakistan to Bhutto, who had gained political legitimacy from his December 1970 election victory.

## Civilian Rule: From 1972 to 1977

Taking over a shrunken and psychologically battered nation, Bhutto demonstrated great leadership skill in rallying his demoralized countrymen. He swiftly clipped the power of the military and sought to shape a democratic constitution. Adopted in 1973, the new basic law replaced the presidential with a parliamentary system. The national assembly elected Bhutto as the prime minister. In line with the PPP's electoral platform, Bhutto implemented a number of socialist economic measures, nationalizing major industries and the banks.

Although he remained popular with the masses, the prime minister began to act increasingly like a feudal autocrat rather than a democratic political leader. He showed little tolerance for opposition inside his own party or from other political groups, established a separate paramilitary security force, politicized the civil service and sent the army into Balochistan to crush tribal unrest. Bhutto also shifted direction in economic policy, adopting more conservative policies and discarding the PPP's leftist approach. Politically, he welcomed large landlords, the traditional power brokers, into the party fold.

18

When Bhutto called for new elections in 1977, the opposition joined forces to mount a surprisingly effective campaign. Although the prime minister stood to win a solid victory, his followers rigged the outcome to ensure a landslide. After the aroused opposition took to the streets, Bhutto found it necessary to seek the army's help in maintaining order. Despite the fact that negotiations with the opposition produced near agreement on new elections, deep mutual mistrust made it difficult for the two sides to seal a final accord. On July 5, 1977, the military intervened, claiming that no end of political unrest was in sight. Bhutto and other political leaders were arrested and martial law once more imposed.

## Return of Military Rule: From 1977 to 1988

The Chief of Army Staff Gen. Zia ul-Haq, who became the country's third martial law administrator, pledged only a temporary stay in power and promised to hold early elections to return Pakistan to civilian rule. Although he shortly released Bhutto and other detained politicians, Zia had the former prime minister rearrested, this time charged with having arranged the murder of a political opponent. Following a lengthy trial and appeal, the courts convicted Bhutto and sentenced him to death. After Zia spurned pleas for clemency from world leaders, including President Jimmy Carter, Bhutto was hanged on April 4, 1979.

In the meanwhile, Zia, who by then had assumed the presidency, kept postponing elections and eventually announced that they would be put off indefinitely. In an effort to gain greater political legitimacy, the unpopular military dictator substantially enlarged the role of Islam in Pakistani life. Under Zia's policy of Islamization, religious courts were established to ensure that all laws were consistent with Islam. The regime also energetically supported the spread of religious schools, or *madrasas*. Zia, nonetheless, remained unpopular at home and abroad because of his harsh rule and the execution of Bhutto.

Moscow's decision to send the Red Army into neighboring

Afghanistan on Christmas Eve 1979 dramatically changed the situation. When Zia publicly opposed the Soviet action and supported the Afghan resistance movement, his international standing rose. The United States and other countries began to provide large amounts of aid and lauded Pakistan's policy. In 1985, after seven years of martial law, Zia allowed renewed political activity and restored the 1973 constitution, which was amended to give the president, not the prime minister, ultimate power. Following elections for a new national assembly, Zia appointed a little known leader from Sindh, Muhammad Khan Junejo, prime minister.

When Junejo surprised the president by refusing to be a puppet, friction developed between the two leaders over their respective roles, over Afghan policy, and over the position of the military. In May 1988, as the Soviets were withdrawing their forces from Afghanistan, Zia fired Junejo, appointed himself prime minister and called for new elections. Three months later, the Zia era ended suddenly when Pakistan's president died in a still unexplained airplane crash that also took the life of American ambassador Arnold L. Raphel.

## Restoration of Civilian Rule: From 1988 to 1999

After the army leadership decided against taking power, Pakistan moved back to the democratic path with elections in November 1988 to choose a new government. The contest was between the political heirs of two men in the grave—Zulfikar Ali Bhutto and his executioner, Zia ul-Haq. When the votes were counted, Bhutto's heir, his charismatic 33-year-old daughter, Benazir, emerged as the victor. Having returned from exile in 1986 to take charge of the PPP, she defeated Zia's heir, Nawaz Sharif, chief minister of the Punjab and the leader of the Pakistan Muslim League (PML).

The promise of a democratic Pakistan that had seemed bright in the fall of 1988 was sadly not realized. During the decade that followed, Bhutto and Sharif alternated in power, each serving twice as prime minister. Neither provided Pakistan with enlightened leadership nor addressed in a sustained fashion the country's growing economic difficulties. Both political leaders seemed more interested in the spoils of power than in good governance.

In August 1990, less than two years after Benazir Bhutto took office, President Ghulam Ishaq Khan, a veteran technocrat, dismissed her, employing the constitutional powers the president had inherited from Zia. Sharif, whom the military and the establishment strongly backed, won the ensuing elections. Although he and Ghulam Ishaq were natural political allies, they managed to become embroiled in a bitter fight that ended in the army's forcing both to resign in mid-1993.

Benazir Bhutto then won a second term as prime minister, defeating Sharif at the polls in October 1993. When she arranged for the election of PPP loyalist Farooq Leghari as president, her position seemed secure. Three years later, nonethe-

AP/Wide World Photos

Jan. 31, 1997: Former Prime Minister Benazir Bhutto (1988–90; 1993–96), ousted from power in November 1996, addresses thousands of supporters in Lokhran, hoping to return to office in February elections. She suffered a withering defeat at the polls.

less, after a falling-out with Leghari over judicial appointments and the conduct of her reportedly corrupt husband, Asif Zardari, Bhutto was dismissed a second time. Nawaz Sharif returned to office with a landslide victory in February 1997 elections. The results were not so much an expression of confidence in Sharif as a vote of "no confidence" in Benazir Bhutto. Sharif quickly strengthened his position by getting the national assembly to amend the constitution to reduce the president's powers and to make the prime minister once more the country's top political figure.

Not content with this action, Sharif also struck at the independence of the judiciary and forced the resignation of Chief of Army Staff Gen. Jehangir Karamat after the latter publicly called for improved governance. Just a year later, on October 12, 1999, Sharif was himself ousted. Karamat's successor, Gen. Pervez Musharraf, had quarreled with the prime minister following the bold but imprudent Pakistani incursion across the "line of control" (dividing Kashmir between territories held by India and Pakistan) in northern Kashmir, near Kargil. When Sharif fired Musharraf, who was then flying back from a visit to Sri Lanka on a commercial airliner, the order was not obeyed and the army instead arrested Sharif. For the fourth time in Pakistan's history, the military was in charge.

In addition to poor governance, both Benazir Bhutto and Nawaz Sharif failed to deal effectively with the upsurge of the Kalashnikov culture (Kalashnikov being the nickname for the AK-47 semiautomatic weapon widely used during the Afghan war), which engulfed Pakistan in the 1990s. Although the country has a tradition of turbulence, especially in the NWFP where carrying guns and honor killings are accepted social norms, the flood of weaponry from the Afghan war helped bring about an unprecedented breakdown in law and order. With arms freely available and the police corrupt and poorly equipped, rival groups were quick to resort to the gun in settling scores and in trying to gain the upper hand. Violent clashes between Sunni and Shia religious militants, previously relatively rare, became an increasingly disturbing feature, especially in the Punjab.

Paul Best, Cartoonists & Writers Syndicate/cartoonweb.com

(Sunnis predominate; Shiites make up about one fifth of Pakistan's Muslims.) Revolutionary Iran reportedly funneled help to the Shia community, while militant Sunni groups received assistance from Saudi Arabia. The increased lawlessness and violence, however, was most striking in Karachi, Pakistan's largest city and commercial and industrial hub. In 1995, more than 2,000 people died in fighting between the Muhajir Quami Mahaz (MQM), Karachi's dominant political party and the representative of refugees from India, and rival groups and government security agencies. During the 1990s, six Americans—two consular officials and four businessmen—were among the victims of Karachi's violence.

## More Military Rule: From 1999–

Unlike Pakistan's three previous military dictators, General Musharraf did not impose martial law, ban political parties or censor the press. Trying to put his best foot forward internationally, Musharraf styled himself Pakistan's chief executive and pledged a purely transitional role for his government.

Although he rebuffed pressure from the United States and the European Union to announce a timetable for the return to democracy, he accepted a ruling by Pakistan's supreme court that the military step down within three years, in other words, not later than October 2002. In June 2001, Musharraf appointed himself president, making clear he intended to remain in power after the election of a new national assembly.

Musharraf, who consults closely with senior generals before making decisions, has used a cabinet composed largely of nonpolitical technocrats. His government has spelled out three main goals: reducing corruption, redressing the country's finances and laying the foundation for more effective and decentralized democratic government. In the effort to stamp out corruption, a number of former high officials and businessmen have been jailed as a means of strengthening accountability. Nawaz Sharif and Benazir Bhutto, who are both in exile, were convicted of financial misdeeds; Sharif, in addition, was found guilty of attempted murder in trying to prevent the aircraft carrying Musharraf, as well as civilian passengers, from landing at Karachi. Although the accountability campaign has made some progress, Musharraf weakened the effort by exempting the military and the judiciary, and by releasing Sharif with a pardon to go into exile in Saudi Arabia.

In trying to put Pakistan's financial house in order, the regime has striven to avoid default on the foreign debt and to broaden the tax base in order to provide sufficient revenue to fund badly needed development and infrastructure projects. The strategy for building a stronger foundation for democracy has focused so far on decentralizing power. Elections on a non-party basis for new local institutions were conducted in stages during the winter and spring of 2001. The new system is scheduled to begin operation on August 14, 2001, the 54th anniversary of Pakistan's independence. Although plans for the government structures at the provincial and national levels have yet to be announced, Musharraf will have to hold elections by the fall of 2002 if his regime heeds the court order to end military rule by then. There is considerable speculation that

24

Musharraf intends to have the constitution revised to once more give the president the authority to dismiss the prime minister.

Musharraf's record during his first year and three quarters in office has been mixed. The army had contingency plans for taking power in the event Sharif tried to remove Musharraf, but it did not have a clear concept of what it would do after gaining power. Although some observers have been highly critical—the October 14, 2000, *Economist* (London) called Musharraf "Pakistan's useless dictator"—the general has persisted in the face of protests from business and commercial interests in pressing ahead with tax reforms, a prerequisite for putting the economy back on the rails. Despite discomfort with sharp criticism by the press, Musharraf has not imposed cen-

**Oct. 13, 1999: Army Chief Pervez Musharraf makes a TV address to the Pakistani nation the day after he overthrew Prime Minister Nawaz Sharif.**

sorship on the media. The overall level of violence has also been reduced: Karachi is once again a relatively calm metropolis.

Musharraf can, however, be faulted for not launching reforms in education and other sectors where Pakistan has fallen way behind. He has also not only failed to rein in Islamic fundamentalists, but under pressure from the religious parties backed off from signing the Comprehensive Test Ban Treaty (prohibiting all nuclear-weapons testing, endorsed by the United Nations in 1996) and from toning down Pakistan's harsh blasphemy laws to make it more difficult for accusers to level charges. In foreign policy, Pakistan continues its official support for the fundamentalist Taliban in Afghanistan while criticizing its extremism and maintains its strong support for the jihad in Kashmir against Indian control.

# 2

# Shaky Institutions

Why has Pakistan experienced such difficulty in developing a stable political system? How is it that India, with as many, if not more, problems, has been able to institutionalize its version of democratic governance? One important factor was that the deaths of Jinnah and Liaqat Ali Khan deprived Pakistan of stable leadership during the critical initial years of independence. Another reason was the early collapse of the Muslim League, a development that left Pakistan without an effective national political party. The senior civil servants and military leaders who filled the political void, such as Iskander Mirza and Ayub Khan, did not believe the country was ready for representative government and considered the politicians incompetent and corrupt. In contrast, Prime Minister Jawaharlal Nehru remained at the helm in India for 17 years after independence. The INC continued to function as the dominant national political organization for nearly half a century. In contrast to Pakistan, the primacy of civilian political leaders over the civil service and the military became firmly established in India.

From the outset, the Pakistani government has been highly centralized and there has been little encouragement for the development of strong local or provincial-level institutions. Most decisions have been made in the capital. The provinces have been largely cash-strapped appendages of the central government. With the executive dominating the stage, neither national nor provincial legislatures have had good records as lawmaking bodies or as arenas for serious policy discussion and debate. Most laws have been promulgated by the executive without parliamentary review.

The history of elected bodies at the local level has been equally discouraging. More often than not, these have been the stepchildren of administrative officials and major landowners, the so-called feudals. It remains to be seen if the local government reforms being initiated by Musharraf will succeed in altering this situation. Strong tribal and clan allegiances also have posed significant barriers to developing a tradition of compromise and give-and-take that is needed to underpin effective representative government. At all levels of government, Pakistan has had a cultural emphasis on the "big leader."

The judiciary has had difficulty in asserting and maintaining its independence. Like the legislatures, the courts have been usually the handmaidens of the executive. For example, the judiciary has been willing to give its after-the-fact blessing to the legality of coups d'état under the doctrine of "state necessity." After taking power in October 1999, Musharraf ensured the loyalty of judges by requiring them to swear an oath of allegiance to the military regime. He retired the roughly 15 percent that refused to do so.

The civil service has played a major role in governing Pakistan. Modeled on the elite Indian Civil Service (ICS) of British India, the Civil Service of Pakistan (CSP) was an elite cadre that occupied key administrative positions until disbanded by Zulfikar Ali Bhutto in the early 1970s. Its less prestigious successor has remained a vital cog in government process but standards of performance have fallen. Pakistan's bureaucracy has gained a reputation for endemic corruption, especially in managing public-sector enterprises and fulfilling discretionary functions, such as the issuance of licenses and permits and collection of taxes and customs duties.

## Political Parties

During the 1990s, the Pakistan People's Party, founded by Zulfikar Ali Bhutto, and the Pakistan Muslim League, the current version of which was sponsored by General Zia ul-Haq and his supporters, alternated in holding power. Although policy differences were narrow, the PPP had a more populist and secular approach while the Muslim League was more conservative and pro-Islamic. Neither party has functioned along democratic lines. Benazir Bhutto was elected chairman for life and still controls the PPP from exile. Nawaz Sharif, who dominated the Muslim League for more than a decade, however, agreed to withdraw from politics for the next 21 years when he accepted exile in Saudi Arabia in December 2000. With Sharif off the political stage, a power struggle is under way between pro- and anti-Sharif factions to gain control of the Muslim League.

Even though the popularity of the two major parties is difficult to measure, their poor performance in office may cut into their support in the next round of national elections which will have to be held by October 2002 if the military follows the court's order. One measure of public discontent has been the steady decline in participation in national elections. After 45.5 percent of those eligible voted in the 1990 election, participation dropped to 40.3 percent in 1993, and then slumped to only 35.9 percent in the 1997 polls. Local elections currently under way are being held on a nonparty basis, but regime spokesmen indicate that political parties will be able to participate in later balloting for provincial and national assemblies.

It is hard to predict the outcome of the next round of voting. The PPP and the Muslim League may demonstrate that they continue to dominate the political scene, but they could also gain less support than in the past. Unless independents or other middle-of-the-road parties, such as those founded by former

29

president Farooq Leghari or cricket star Imran Khan, are able to attract significant public backing, the beneficiaries could be the religious parties. In the past, these have fared poorly at the ballot box, rarely winning more than 5 percent of the vote, and gaining few seats in the provincial and national assemblies. The best-known Islamic group is the Jamaat-i-Islami, which was founded by renowned cleric Maulana Maududi. Along with other fundamentalist parties, the Jamaat has gained influence and legitimacy through official patronage during the Zia era and in the years since then. During the Afghan war (1979–89), the Inter Services Intelligence (ISI) directorate used the religious parties and their affiliates as vehicles for funneling arms and other supplies to resistance groups. Similarly, in recent years, the ISI has cooperated with Islamic factions and their armed affiliates in fanning the flames of the anti-India insurgency in Kashmir and in supporting the Taliban in Afghanistan.

Despite their unimpressive showing at the polls, the fundamentalists have demonstrated the capability to mobilize street demonstrations and have become an important political pressure group. The Jamaat, in particular, has vocally criticized Musharraf, although not the military. The religious parties take a hardline anti-India and anti-United States stance and call for greater Islamization of Pakistani society and life. The country's problems, they claim, stem from the ruling elite's having followed Western norms rather than having adopted Islam as the guide. Their approach varies from the more moderate parties such as the Jamaat-i-Islami to extreme groups that want to impose a strict Islamic code. Until now, Pakistan has been ruled primarily by the English-speaking elite, whether civilian or military. Were the religious parties to gain a more important voice in government, this could change significantly, as they draw their support mainly from urban lower middle classes and have few ties with the elite.

## Imbalance between the Provinces

The imbalance between the Punjab and the other provinces has been a major source of political difficulty. Containing roughly two thirds of the population, providing the bulk of Pakistan's armed forces, and possessing the most productive agricultural land, the Punjab has loomed large in the eyes of other provinces. This preponderance has triggered resentment that has assumed an ethnic character, since provincial boundaries in the main correspond to the country's major ethnic divisions.

Sindh, the second-most populous province and the home of Zulfikar Ali Bhutto and his daughter Benazir, has a history of grievances against the more developed and prosperous Punjab. Sindhis claim to have been discriminated against in the allocation of development funds. They also complain that Punjabis have taken up much of the land that new irrigation projects have made available for agricultural production. Rivalry between Urdu-speaking refugees from India, the Muhajir community—in effect, Pakistan's fifth ethnic group—and native Sindhis has also embittered political life in the province. The major refugee party, the MQM, has dominated the city of Karachi even though its leader, Altaf Hussain, has been in exile in Britain for nearly a decade.

There has been less friction between the Punjab and the NWFP, which borders on Afghanistan and is the home for most Pashtuns (Pathans). As in the days of the British Raj, customary tribal law rather than normal Pakistani law and administration prevails in a large part of the province. The NWFP's population has grown rapidly in recent years with the influx of several million refugees from the Afghan war. Some have gone home, but many of them have become assimilated into Pakistan, especially around the provincial capital of Peshawar.

In the southwest, thinly peopled Balochistan is mostly arid desert or mountain terrain. Its population is divided between native Balochis and southern Pashtuns. The latter have gained in political influence as their numbers have been swollen by Afghan refugees, many around the capital city of Quetta. Balochistan has remained a largely tribal society, one which has a long history of friction with the central government, including a serious insurgency in the 1970s. During the Afghan war, the province provided a home for many Islamic madrasas, including those linked with the conservative Deobandi sect, which became the major seedbed for the Taliban movement.

# 3

# The Pakistani Military

THE NATIONAL SECURITY threat that Pakistanis perceive from India has dominated defense thinking ever since independence. The fact that war broke out over Kashmir in October 1947 made building up the military a top priority. The new nation had a strong martial tradition and an ample pool of manpower  Punjabi Muslims were the largest single group of soldiers in the British Indian army. But Pakistan lacked the arms and equipment, financial resources and industrial capacity to underpin a significant defense establishment.

## *Unsteady Alliance with the Americans*

In 1954, the leadership in Karachi thought it had found a solution to this problem by becoming a military ally of the United States. During the next decade, the Americans provided over half a billion dollars worth of arms assistance, helping Pakistan develop a defense force that although smaller in size than India's was better equipped and better trained. An important by-product of the inflow of U.S. aid was the enhancement of the army's political influence, even though political events in Karachi would probably not have unfolded very differently had the United States not decided to provide Pakistan with military aid.

The supply of U.S. arms was interrupted by the 1965 war with India. China stepped in to become Pakistan's principal arms source, but Beijing lacked the wherewithal to fully replace Washington. Defeat by India in the 1971 war further degraded the military's capability and sapped its confidence. Bhutto and then Zia gradually rebuilt conventional defense forces and also launched a secret program to develop a nuclear-weapons capability to match the one that India had demonstrated in its May 1974 test.

The Afghan war provided a great boost to the armed forces. Pakistan once more received substantial quantities of American military equipment, including the powerful F-16 fighter-bomber. Even though the secret nuclear program caused chronic friction with U.S. efforts to prevent the further spread of nuclear weapons, Pakistan persisted and by the late 1980s was able to acquire a nuclear-weapons capability.

In 1990, the flow of U.S. military assistance stopped once again. After the intelligence community had firmly concluded that Pakistan possessed a nuclear weapon, Washington imposed sanctions mandated under the Pressler amendment to the foreign assistance act, which required the President to certify annually that Pakistan did not possess a nuclear explosive device. The suspension of arms aid, which was then running about $300 million annually, was a severe blow to Pakistan's military. Given the economic straits that the country faced during the 1990s, finding financial resources to maintain the defense forces proved difficult. Nonetheless, military spending has continued at a high level. In 1997, defense took 28 percent of the central government's budget and represented 5.9 percent of Pakistan's gross national product (GNP).

In view of Pakistan's difficulty in maintaining its conventional force capability, nuclear weapons, which are controlled by the army, have assumed great importance as a deterrent against India. From Pakistan's strategic perspective, official support for the Taliban has been a way to gain "strategic depth"

Pakistan Day, March 23, 1999: A Pakistani-made Ghauri surface-to-surface missile rolls past a portrait of Muhammad Ali Jinnah, Pakistan's founder. The Ghauri, which can carry nuclear warheads, has a range of 930 miles and is capable of reaching targets in most of India.

©AFP/CORBIS

against India by ensuring a friendly government in Afghanistan, one which is dominated by fellow Pashtuns. Apart from a desire to pay India back for its "dismembering" of Pakistan in the 1971 war, support for the ongoing insurgency in Kashmir has had appeal for military strategists as a low-cost way of tying down several hundred thousand Indian soldiers in a "dirty war" that has tarnished India's international image and has so far run little military risk for Pakistan.

## Reputation of the Military Remains High

The defense establishment continues to have a reputation for functioning efficiently and for professional and organizational integrity. The military has maintained a strong corporate identity and a sense of esprit as the "defender of the Pakistan ideology." By Pakistani standards, the services take excellent care of their people, whether on active duty or retired. In the early years, the officer corps came mainly from wealthier landlord families, but the urban middle class has become increasingly important as a source of personnel. Although the army has been able to maintain the regimental traditions passed on from the British Indian army, there has been greater emphasis on Islam since the Zia years. The extent to which the current military is "secular" or "Islamic" remains a much-debated topic. Over the past two decades, many military officers have worked closely with Islamic extremist groups in the "holy-war" struggles in Afghanistan and Kashmir, and they presumably share at least some of the views of the fundamentalists.

## *Role of the ISI*

There has been much controversy over the role and power of the Inter Services Intelligence directorate, which successfully managed the Afghan war, working closely with the U.S. Central Intelligence Agency (CIA), and more recently has supported the Taliban's rise to power in Afghanistan and the anti-India jihad in Kashmir. The ISI is staffed both by career civilian intelligence specialists and military officers on temporary assignment. The head of the intelligence agency, the director-general, has traditionally been an army general who is appointed by the head of government, to whom the ISI chief, in theory, reports. Even though the ISI technically stands outside of the chain of command, the fact that its chief and a considerable portion of the staff are serving officers gives the army leadership a strong voice in ISI operations. (When Benazir Bhutto sought to gain control of the ISI in 1989 by appointing a retired general as director-general, the army was able to render her appointee ineffective.)

Like the CIA, the ISI has responsibility for gathering intelligence from abroad and for carrying out covert-action operations outside the borders of Pakistan. However, since Zulfikar Ali Bhutto expanded the ISI's mandate in the mid-1970s, it has been authorized to carry on intelligence activities inside Pakistan as well. In this capacity, the ISI has become an active and destabilizing factor in the domestic political process. For example, the ISI promoted the political opposition to Benazir Bhutto's first government and actively supported Nawaz Sharif's 1988 and 1990 election campaigns. Unless action is taken to trim ISI's domestic role, this will remain a negative element in Pakistani politics, making it harder to establish stable and representative government.

## *Military Rule: Mixed Record*

For over half of Pakistan's first 54 years of independence, the military has ruled the country. Only when Jinnah and Liaqat led Pakistan from 1947 until 1951, and Zulfikar Ali Bhutto during the early 1970s, has the military been subject to civilian control. At other times, even when not actually in power, as in the mid-1950s and the 1990s, the military has played an important political role. This has ranged from blatant interference in elections to more subtle behind-the-scenes activity. The army, which currently has about 500,000 men, has always been the major component of the armed forces and has exerted by far the most political influence. The smaller air force and tiny navy have had much less to say.

During the most recent period of civilian rule in the 1990s, the relationship between military and civilian leaders was uneasy much of the time. Prime Ministers Benazir Bhutto and Nawaz Sharif were constantly looking over their shoulders to see what the army was up to. For their part, the military leaders have tended to view civilian leaders and politicians with disdain and have been able to insist on having the final word over key national security matters, such as policy on Kashmir, Afghanistan and nuclear issues.

Yet, despite the army's reputation for efficiency, the military has not done a much better job of running Pakistan than the civilians. Ayub Khan was by far the best military ruler, but stayed on too long and made a major strategic error in getting into the 1965 war with India. Yahya Khan, who presided over the East Pakistan disaster, was tragically beyond his depth. Although Zia ul-Haq was a shrewd operator who managed to remain in power for over a decade without much popular support, his legacy was on the whole negative. His Afghan policy brilliantly succeeded against the Soviets, but its consequences have been woeful—another decade of war and destruction in Afghanistan and a surge of lawlessness, increased drug use and Islamic fundamentalism in Pakistan. Moreover, Zia failed to take advantage of Pakistan's relative prosperity during the 1980s to address underlying socioeconomic problems. Finally, although Zia put Pakistan back on the path of representative government in 1985, he proved unwilling in the end to relinquish power to civilian leaders.

The jury remains out on Pervez Musharraf. As of midyear 2001, he and his senior colleagues seem to recognize that a purely military regime does not have the answers to Pakistan's problems, but at the same time they are skeptical about the ability of the politicians to lead the country effectively. Musharraf's action to appoint himself president was one indication of this line of thinking. It is also widely expected that the 1973 constitution will be modified to give the president the power to dismiss an elected prime minister, a power that Zia and his successors possessed from 1985 until 1997. Another frequently discussed way of giving the military a continuing role in governance would be the creation of some sort of national security council that would include both military and civilian leaders, modeled broadly speaking on Turkey. Critics argue that this step, along with stronger presidential powers, would impair democratically elected leadership. Supporters believe such a body would provide needed stability and better balance to the government process.

# 4

# Uneven Economic
# and Social Development

THE ECONOMIC challenges that Pakistan faced in 1947
were as daunting as those in the political and administrative spheres. Both eastern and western parts of the country had largely agricultural economies. Transportation and communication links were poor. Industry was virtually nonexistent. Among the few pluses were two significant cash crops, jute in the east and cotton in the west, and modern port facilities in Karachi. Agriculture in the Punjab and in Sindh also benefited from one of the world's largest irrigation systems, which tapped the Indus River and its tributaries in the Punjab. Although some small landowners existed, large holdings were the rule, especially in Sindh and in much of the Punjab. Some landlords, or feudals as they were called, controlled vast estates and dominated rural society much as landlords had in nineteenth-century czarist Russia.

Initially after independence, economic life continued unchanged. The borders with India were open and trade flowed freely, as if the two countries remained a single economic unit.

This situation ended in 1949 after India devalued its rupee currency to match the devaluation of the British pound sterling, and Pakistan decided not to follow suit. When India responded by banning trade rather than paying more for Pakistani goods, the central government in Karachi spurred the development of indigenous manufacturing industries. Thanks to the sharp rise in commodity prices during the Korean War (1950–53), earnings from jute and cotton exports provided the foreign exchange needed to fund Pakistan's rapid industrial expansion. Over a hundred textile mills sprang up, mainly around Karachi, to process cotton grown in the Indus Valley, which had formerly been exported to India. In the east wing, numerous mills were also established to process jute, which had been previously shipped to Calcutta.

After the Korean War boom petered out in 1952–53, the economy slumped badly. The situation was aggravated by poor macroeconomic planning, political instability, neglect of agricultural development and the related loss of large tracts of irrigated land in the west to water logging and salinity. By the time Pakistan became an ally of the United States in 1954, its economy was in dire straits. Fortunately, Washington was willing to bolster its new security partner with substantial amounts of financial help and food aid. American economists associated with the Harvard Development Advisory Service and the Ford Foundation also worked in harness with Pakistani counterparts in shaping economic policy. From its inception, Pakistan— in contrast to India—followed a free-market-oriented approach favoring private-sector development and did not pursue the then fashionable policy of developing a large state-managed public sector.

## Economy Improves under Ayub

After Ayub Khan took power in October 1958, he entrusted direction of the economy to Finance Minister Muhammad Shoaib, a respected World Bank official. Within a couple of years, greater political stability, steadier economic policies and increased foreign assistance inflows turned the country around.

From near stagnation, Pakistan's GNP began to grow at an annual rate of better than 5 percent. The bulk of foreign assistance flowed to West Pakistan, where the economic prospects were considered relatively brighter than in the poorer east wing. This policy fueled increasing discontent among Bengalis, who charged that the West Pakistan–dominated central government was discriminating against them. Even though East Pakistani jute exports, the complaint went, generated much of the country's foreign-exchange earnings, the province received an unfairly small share of development funds.

In the first half of the 1960s, Pakistan's economic performance continued to be robust. The GNP increased an average of 5.2 percent annually and rose from $8.5 billion to $10.1 billion between fiscal years 1963 and 1965, an impressive 9.4 percent rate of annual growth. The United States provided roughly $400 million worth of foreign assistance a year—$200 million in economic aid, $160 million in food aid and $40 million in military assistance. Pakistan was then regarded as a potentially major foreign-aid success story; the U.S. Agency for International Development even brought economists from South Korea to study the Pakistani model of development.

By 1965, indeed, Pakistan seemed to be close to attaining self-sustainable growth, a remarkable achievement for a country that had been in desperate economic straits just a decade before. The Ayub government hoped to double development expenditures to $10.9 billion during the following five years and to maintain a respectable annual growth rate of 6.5 percent of GNP. Moreover, major initiatives to improve population control, health and education were planned to overcome admitted weaknesses in these areas.

## Negative Impact of Indo-Pakistani Conflicts

Regrettably for Pakistan, political problems slowed the advance of the economy. Upset over the U.S. decision to give military aid to India after the 1962 Sino-Indian border conflict, Ayub angered President Lyndon B. Johnson (1963–69) by moving Pakistan closer to China. The annoyed U.S. President responded by putting off a visit by Ayub in April 1965 and then forcing the postponement of the World Bank–sponsored pledging session of the aid-to-Pakistan consortium. After war broke out with India in September 1965, Johnson suspended both military and economic aid to Pakistan (and also India). Although economic, but not military, assistance was resumed after the war ended, the disruption in the aid flow and the costs of the conflict badly set back Pakistan's economy.

Still, the outlook remained positive in the late 1960s. Pakistan was beginning to enjoy increased food-grain production thanks to the green revolution in agriculture. However, political unrest that forced Ayub from office in 1969 upset the economy once more. Two years later, the crisis over East Pakistan and the ensuing war with India further aggravated the situation. Although shrunken and shaken, Pakistan was able, nonetheless, to ride out the impact of the sharp rise in fuel prices after the 1973 oil crisis, thanks to increased financial assistance from Saudi Arabia, Iran and other Middle East oil producers. Foreign-exchange remittances from Pakistanis who found employment in the Persian Gulf also provided a considerable assist.

Forward movement of the economy, however, once more slowed after Bhutto implemented socialist policies that he had advocated during the 1970 election campaign. His nationalization of major industries, commercial banks and life insurance companies resulted in the creation of a substantial public sector and a serious loss of business confidence. Control of important parts of the economy passed to the hands of civil servants with a corresponding rise in inefficiency and corruption. In retrospect, Bhutto's leftist economic policies proved a major turning point that set back Pakistan's longer-term economic prospects. Industrial growth, which had risen at an annual rate of 9.1 percent during the 1960s, slipped to 2.3 percent a year during the 1970s.

## Better Economic Times in the 1980s

After Zia ul-Haq overthrew Bhutto in 1977, he sought to revive the market-oriented policies of the Ayub era, but did not denationalize public-sector industries, banks and insurance companies. Zia also appointed many senior military officers to important administrative posts as a form of patronage. Although in the 1990s, Zia's successors, Benazir Bhutto and Nawaz Sharif, favored the private sector, neither undertook a serious effort to privatize public-sector enterprises. These have remained inefficient, overstaffed and a drain on government finances, as well as a chronic source of corruption. Government-run banks, in particular, made numerous politically motivated and economically unsound loans, in the process weakening the viability of Pakistan's financial institutions.

During the 1980s, remittances from several million Pakistanis working in the Persian Gulf and the positive financial fallout from the Afghan war gave the economy a major boost. As the key partner in combating the Soviet military presence in Afghanistan, Pakistan received substantially increased foreign aid, along with help in supporting several million Afghan refugees. Beginning in 1982, the United States, the World Bank, the Asian Development Bank, as well as Saudi Arabia, Japan and West European countries, boosted their financial help to Pakistan.

The 1980s saw a significant reduction in poverty and a substantial rise in living standards. The GNP grew at an annual rate of 6.3 percent. The country enjoyed a renewed spurt of industrialization, especially among small- and medium-sized industries. Employment possibilities in the Persian Gulf eased the strains caused by the burgeoning population. Unfortunately, the Zia regime failed to tackle Pakistan's human infrastructure shortcomings at a time when economic circumstances were relatively favorable. Moreover, high tax rates and endemic corruption spurred widespread tax evasion. A large black market developed, especially in mid-sized enterprises and industries, depriving the government of substantial resources. Nor did Zia move to increase revenues by taxing agricultural income, preferring to leave the earnings of the "feudals" untouched. Despite the impressive rate of growth throughout the 1980s, there was insufficient "trickle down" for Pakistan to cross the threshold into the status of a middle-income country.

## Economy Slumps in the 1990s

After the Red Army withdrew from Afghanistan in 1988–89, the economic outlook worsened. Foreign assistance, much of which was politically motivated by the Afghan war, declined. The heaviest blow came in 1990 when the United States suspended its $574 million military and economic assistance program because of Pakistan's nuclear-weapons program. Overall, foreign aid inflows dropped from $10 per capita, or 2.7 percent of GNP, in 1990 to $5 per capita, or only one percent of GNP in 1997. A decline in worker remittances from the Persian Gulf also hurt the economy during the 1990s.

Benazir Bhutto and Nawaz Sharif proved to be undisciplined economic managers. When tax collection proved inadequate to fund projected expenditures, both resorted to heavy short-term borrowing from abroad to fill the gap. By 1997, servicing the debt had become the largest item in government expenditure; external debt had ballooned to $29.7 billion, or 38 percent of GNP. (In contrast, in 1997, India's foreign debt was 18 percent of GNP and Bangladesh's 20 percent.) Coupled with defense spending, heavy debt-service outlays left few funds for health, education and social programs, or for maintenance of the country's physical infrastructure. Pakistan's road, railroad and telecommunications systems suffered significant deterioration.

Although Nawaz Sharif came from a business family and advocated a more market-oriented approach than Benazir Bhutto, he had a penchant for costly projects of questionable economic value. During his first term as prime minister (1990–93), Sharif introduced an expensive populist scheme of importing small taxicabs that were then sold at subsidized prices. In his second term (1997–99), Sharif made the construction of a modern, but expensive, six-lane superhighway between Lahore and Islamabad a top priority. Although the roadway reduced driving time between the two cities, high tolls put it beyond the reach of most Pakistanis.

During the 1990s, Pakistan was in near nonstop negotiation with the International Monetary Fund (IMF) in order to obtain structural-adjustment loans to stave off debt default and potential national bankruptcy. In return for new financial assistance, the IMF required Pakistan to reduce its budget deficit, to increase tax revenues and to move ahead more vigorously with the privatization of state-owned industries and businesses. Islamabad did just enough to keep the IMF happy but failed to implement the reforms in a wholehearted manner. Rampant corruption aggravated economic problems. It was widely believed that Benazir Bhutto's husband, whom the prime minister astoundingly appointed minister for investment in 1996, regularly received a rake-off on government contracts.

The power sector, however, was one area where Bhutto acted forcefully. In an effort to overcome chronic electricity shortages, numerous foreign companies, including several from the United States, agreed to build power plants. The contracts were backed by Pakistan's sovereign guarantee. When Nawaz Sharif returned to office in 1997, he voided most of the agreements, notwithstanding the sovereign guarantee, on the grounds that they were tainted by bribes and corruption. The result was to worsen Pakistan's already poor reputation as a safe haven for foreign investment.

The economic situation reached the crisis stage in May 1998 after the United States and other major industrial powers imposed fresh sanctions following Pakistan's nuclear-weapons tests. Fears that the punishment might sink the shaky economy were not misplaced. At the time Pakistan tested its nuclear capability, its foreign debt was over $30 billion while foreign-exchange reserves were only $600 million. When a panicky Nawaz Sharif froze foreign-currency bank accounts after the tests, the action created havoc for foreign companies working in Pakistan. Growing increasingly anxious about possible financial collapse, Washington decided to provide Islamabad some breathing room and relaxed opposition to IMF financial assistance. After lengthy negotiations, the Pakistanis and the IMF agreed on yet another economic program— more of a bandage to prevent the economy from going under than a comprehensive attack on Pakistan's economic ills.

## Musharraf Pledges Reforms

Hopes for improvement rose after the military ousted Nawaz Sharif in October 1999. Musharraf pledged to make financial and economic reform a top priority and appointed Shauhat Aziz, a respected Citibank official, as finance minister. The record has been reasonably positive even though agricultural production has been hit by drought. Islamabad and the IMF agreed on a new stabilization program in November 2000 after extended negotiations. Clamping down on corruption has not proven an easy task, but a start has been made. With the culture of bribery deeply entrenched, the anticorruption campaign has tended to worsen an already poor business climate. Along with increasing "accountability," improving tax collection and introducing a general sales tax, a task that neither Zia, Benazir Bhutto, nor Nawaz Sharif was able to accomplish, have become litmus tests for the Musharraf regime's economic performance. Indeed, unless Pakistan can increase substantially revenue generation through a wider tax net and more effective collection, it will not be able to create sufficient funds to improve its human and physical infrastructure. Here, too, progress has been made even though revenue receipts remain below targets. To help this effort, the World Bank approved a $350 million loan to bolster the tax system.

## Education Achievements Uneven

Pakistan inherited a government-run education system that was modest in scope and almost entirely urban. At independence, the vast majority of Pakistanis who lived in rural areas had almost no access to schooling. After Ayub Khan took power in 1958, Pakistan began to address its educational and other social deficiencies in a serious manner, but first the 1965 war and the related economic development slowdown and then domestic turmoil between 1969 and 1971 diverted energy and sapped funds from human development programs. In the 1970s, Zulfikar Ali Bhutto called for a more egalitarian approach and nationalized private schools and colleges. His action led to reduced standards without improving the overall availability of education. When Gen. Zia ul-Haq took power, he reversed Bhutto's policy and once more permitted privately run schools, where English was the language of instruction. Since then, these have prospered as middle- and upper-class Pakistanis, largely urban dwellers, have sought better educational opportunities for their children.

At the same time, as part of his policy of promoting Islamization, Zia encouraged the spread of religious schools where the Quran and conservative religious values formed the core of the curriculum. With government backing, thousands of madrasas have sprung up, catering mainly to poorer students in urban and rural areas. These schools have ignored math, science and other secular subjects and focused almost entirely on religious education. Some have had close links with Islamic fundamentalists and have become breeding grounds for extremists, training students for holy war and nurturing the Taliban movement.

Over the years, what amounts to a two-track system of primary and secondary education has developed. One track comprises the English-language private schools, which cater to the urban middle and upper classes and follow a curriculum linked to British standards. The second track provides schooling for the poor majority, which has to choose between the Islamic madrasas or underfunded and inadequate government-run schools which largely teach in Urdu. As Pakistan's appalling literacy figures indicate, the availability of schooling at the primary level is still far from universal. Even though spending on education rose from 2 percent to 3 percent of GNP between 1980 and 1996, this lagged below the average of 3.9 percent for all low-income countries. Pakistan continues to spend twice as much on defense as on its schools.

At the upper end of the education ladder, Punjab University in Lahore was the sole institution of higher learning in 1947, although there were a number of well-regarded colleges, mainly in major cities and often run by missionaries. Since then, the university system has expanded rapidly and Pakistan currently has several dozen institutions of higher learning. Greater quantity has unfortunately paralleled a decline in the quality of university education. If Pakistanis can afford to do so, they send their children abroad to study at the college and graduate school level. By the 1970s, the United States had replaced Britain as the favored destination. Many Pakistani students have remained in the United States after graduation to form the backbone of the rapidly growing Pakistani-American ethnic community, estimated at over 300,000.

## Inadequate Medical and Population Programs

In 1947, access to health care, like education, was limited. Government hospitals were found in the cities, alongside private, mostly missionary-run, medical facilities. Some medical care was available in smaller towns, but almost none in the countryside. After the economy began to move ahead briskly in the early 1960s, the Ayub government launched a major program to expand and improve medical facilities. Progress has been uneven. Between 1971 and 1991, the number of doctors increased sixfold and the number of hospital beds more than doubled. But the growth has been mainly in urban areas. Although two thirds of Pakistan's population continue to live in the countryside, five sixths of hospital beds and physicians are found in cities and towns.

Like other developing countries, Pakistan has been successful in reducing the incidence of previously endemic diseases, such as malaria, cholera, typhoid and intestinal ailments. This has led to a sharp decline in the death rate which, however, has not been matched by a corresponding decline in the birthrate. The result has been a quadrupling of Pakistan's population from 32 million in 1947 in the then western part of the country to 151 million, as estimated by the Population Reference Bureau in mid-2000. During the 1990s, the annual growth rate was 2.8 percent, or about 3.5 million people a year. In contrast, the growth rate of Bangladesh's population dipped to 1.9 percent and India's to 2.0 percent during the same period. When it was part of Pakistan, Bangladesh's population was larger than that of West Pakistan; today the tables have been reversed.

During the Ayub Khan years, Pakistan launched a large family-planning effort. Although progress was made, the program encountered resistance, especially in rural areas where children have been traditionally regarded as a form of social insurance. Some Muslim clerics also opposed family planning as contrary to the teachings of Islam. Over the years, the relative neglect of female education has been a further impediment. Lack of policy continuity and stability in administering the population-control program has posed another serious problem. In the 1960s, the use of intrauterine devices was stressed. In the 1970s, emphasis shifted to flooding the country with free contraceptives. By the mid-1980s, the program's focus had changed again, this time to provision of family-planning services through local health clinics. In the 1990s, the policy thrust shifted once more, making the family-welfare program the main vehicle to promote population control.

## Disappointing Human Development Record

In addressing basic human needs, Pakistan's performance over the past half century has been disappointing. In 1998, for example, 42 percent of males above 15 years of age could still neither read nor write and a shocking 71 percent of females remained illiterate. Some 50 million Pakistanis, or nearly one third of the entire population, lacked access to even rudimentary health care. Pakistan's population of just over 150 million remains among the fastest growing of the larger developing countries.

In retrospect, it is a tragedy that the human development programs begun in the Ayub years were not vigorously carried forward by his successors. The Zia regime, in particular, can be faulted for not capitalizing on Pakistan's relative prosperity during the 1980s to launch a sustained and broad-gauged thrust to promote education, health and family planning. In the 1990s, there was much discussion about enhancing human development, but inadequate funding and poor program implementation. The Musharraf government, like its predecessors, has talked a good game but has shown limited urgency in addressing Pakistan's social-sector deficiencies.

The human-development challenges facing Pakistan at the beginning of the twenty-first century are daunting. The failure to do a better job in education, health and family planning has cost the country dearly and will be difficult to overcome in the short term. As the information revolution moves into high gear, the majority of Pakistanis have been left behind, unable to read or write, let alone use computers or the Internet.

# 5

# Pakistan's Relations
# with Its Neighbors

NOT SURPRISINGLY, given the nature and trauma of partition, relations with India have been the central focus of Pakistan's foreign policy concerns. Dividing the British Raj's financial and physical assets, settling refugee property claims, deciding how to share vital irrigation water and demarcating borders were enormous tasks. But above all, the psychological scars left by splitting India into two countries–the suffering and pain of millions of people who fled their homes for an uncertain future—made the establishment of normal ties far harder and have left a legacy of deep mutual distrust. To make matters worse, the dispute over the princely state of Jammu and Kashmir erupted into war in October 1947. During the past half century, differences over Kashmir have provided a chronic flash point to worsen and embitter relations.

## The Kashmir Dispute

The origins of this dispute lay in the hasty breakup of the British Raj in 1947. There was simply not enough time to sort out all the thorny problems, including the fate of the major Indian princely states. Theoretically independent when the British left, the 564 principalities were pressed to join either India or Pakistan depending on their physical location and the communal makeup of their populations. By mid-August 1947, almost all had decided one way or the other, but unfortunately the two largest princely states—Hyderabad and Kashmir—had failed to do so. Located in the center of India, Hyderabad had a Muslim ruler and a predominantly Hindu population. New Delhi forcibly absorbed the state in September 1948. Kashmir, a state that bordered on both countries and lay in the extreme north of the subcontinent, posed the opposite dilemma; it had a Hindu ruler and a Muslim-majority population.

Because of its largely Muslim character and the fact that transportation links were entirely with Pakistan, observers expected that Kashmir eventually would join Pakistan. But the ruler, an unpopular and despotic maharajah, wavered, taking no decision before independence came in August 1947. Unrest soon broke out in the western part of the state where Muslim veterans of the British Indian army proclaimed Azad (or Free) Kashmir and sought to overthrow the maharajah. In late October 1947, several thousand Pashtun tribesmen were bussed into Kashmir from Pakistan's NWFP to join the rebels. Although the Pakistan government may not have organized the incursion, its officials were clearly involved. As the tribals advanced rapidly toward Srinagar, the maharajah's forces disintegrated. At this point, the panicked ruler signed the document of accession to India which New Delhi accepted on the condition that Kashmir's ultimate fate would be resolved by "reference to the people" (i.e., a plebiscite). India was able to fly in sufficient troops to stop the advance of the tribesmen, who had failed to capture the airport at Srinagar, the only possible point of entry for Indian forces.

After bilateral talks did not succeed in resolving the dispute,

India took the issue to the UN in January 1948. In the spring, the Security Council adopted a resolution calling for the withdrawal of all forces and a plebiscite to decide the future of Kashmir. Fighting continued, however, until a UN-brokered cease-fire went into effect on January 1, 1949. With minor modifications, the cease-fire line established then has remained the dividing line between the parts of the state that India and Pakistan control. Over the next decade and a half, there were strenuous efforts by the UN, the United States and Britain to help find a Kashmir solution. Perhaps the primary obstacle to reaching a settlement was the emotional attachment of Indian Prime Minister Nehru to Kashmir. The Nehru family came from the Srinagar valley and belonged to a Kashmiri Brahmin caste.

The last sustained effort at resolving the dispute came after the Sino-Indian border conflict in the Himalayas in October–November 1962. Prodded by Washington and London, New Delhi and Islamabad agreed to negotiations and held six rounds of talks that ultimately failed. India indicated willingness to accept the cease-fire line, with some adjustments in Pakistan's favor, as the international border. Pakistan insisted on a plebiscite in the valley although it was prepared to accept the cease-fire line to the north and south of the valley as the boundary. When the Americans and British proposed partition of the valley or what amounted to a soft border policy, both the Indians and Pakistanis said no.

## 1965 Kashmir War

In mid-1965, frustrated by the failure to resolve the dispute and fearful of Pakistan's losing its military edge over India, Ayub Khan agreed to a bold but poorly conceived plan called Operation Gibraltar. The idea, strongly supported by then Foreign Minister Zulfikar Ali Bhutto, was to infiltrate guerrillas into India's portion of Kashmir in the hope that they would foment sufficient trouble that India would feel compelled to come to the negotiating table. The guerrilla effort fizzled, but triggered full-scale war when India struck back across the international frontier. Bitter fighting raged near the city of Lahore for over two weeks before a cease-fire took effect. Although the conflict was a military standoff, India won by not losing. Pakistan failed to gain Kashmir and in the process lost U.S. military assistance.

In 1971, the two countries went to war again, this time over East Pakistan, not Kashmir. The result was a humiliating Pakistani defeat, the surrender of 93,000 troops and the creation of Bangladesh. After the war, Zulfikar Ali Bhutto, who succeeded the disgraced military dictator Gen. Yahya Khan, agreed with India's Prime Minister Indira Gandhi in meetings at Shimla, the mountain resort in the Himalayas, to solve disputes bilaterally—something India had long sought. The cease-fire line was transformed into a "line of actual control" that Indian and Pakistani military teams mapped on the ground.

For a decade and a half, until 1989, the Kashmir issue remained on the back burner. A weakened Pakistan was in no position to challenge India during the 1970s. Later, during the Afghan war years of the 1980s, President Zia believed it was unwise to stir up the issue and face trouble on both eastern and western frontiers. In addition, the fact that India permitted the popular Kashmiri leader Sheikh Abdullah, whom Nehru had jailed in 1953, to return to power in 1973 eased tensions within the state.

## Kashmir Uprising

The Kashmir dispute might have remained semidormant had internal unrest in India's part of the state not erupted in 1989. The source of the discontent was the frustration of Kashmiri youth over rigged state elections—only the 1977 polls were considered genuinely free—and over New Delhi's blatant interference in local affairs following the death of Sheikh Abdullah in 1982. Angered by their inability to voice grievances peacefully, Muslim Kashmiri youth began to express their feelings through violent means. The Palestinian *intifada*, or uprising, and the Afghan jihad provided models for an armed struggle against India. Pakistan's ISI, which had mastered guerrilla techniques during the Afghan war, was only too happy to assist what had

54

Oct. 24, 1997: Thousands of Pakistanis of every political stripe join hands on the road to the India-Pakistan border in a protest over India's rule over part of Kashmir.

begun as an indigenous uprising. The ISI funneled arms and other aid through Islamic fundamentalist groups much as it had done in combating the Soviets in Afghanistan.

The international community, including the United States, did not react as strongly as it had in the 1950s and 1960s, and initially limited its diplomatic involvement to urging both sides to find a way to resolve the Kashmir dispute. Pakistan's call for third-party mediation fell on deaf ears, while India's indiscriminate and large-scale use of repressive force drew international criticism. After India and Pakistan tested nuclear weapons in 1998, however, the world, especially the United States, began to pay increased attention to Kashmir. President Bill Clinton expressed concern that the ongoing dispute could slip out of control and threaten the nightmare scenario of a nuclear exchange between India and Pakistan.

In February 1999, Indian Prime Minister Atal Bihari Vajpayee visited Lahore to reopen India-Pakistan bus service and joined Nawaz Sharif in pledging a sustained effort to improve bilateral relations. The spirit of Lahore proved short-lived, however. Just three months later, Pakistani-supported insurgents crossed the line of control to threaten Indian positions in the mountainous northern part of Kashmir, near the town of Kargil. When an angry New Delhi forcefully counterattacked, a worried United States urged Pakistan to withdraw the forces rather than risk a wider conflict. At a hurriedly arranged July 4, 1999, meeting in Washington with President Clinton, Prime Minister Nawaz Sharif endorsed the pullback. The failed Kargil operation, however, resulted in no slackening of Pakistani support for the insurgency. Since General Musharraf assumed power in October 1999, Pakistan has continued to back holy war in Kashmir against India. Tensions were lessened somewhat after India announced a unilateral cease-fire late in November 2000 and Pakistan responded by reducing artillery and mortar firing from its side, but the insurgency has continued.

On May 23, 2001, India announced that it was ending the unilateral cease-fire in Kashmir, but Prime Minister Vajpayee invited Pakistan's military ruler, General Musharraf, to visit India and restart negotiations. On May 29, Musharraf formally accepted India's invitation and their summit meetings in Agra in July mark a renewed effort by the two countries to reduce tensions.

In December 1962, after visiting India and Pakistan, veteran American diplomat W. Averell Harriman told President John F. Kennedy that the bar to solving the Kashmir dispute was that any settlement that India would accept would be unacceptable to Pakistan and vice versa. Four decades later, Harriman's words still ring true. In recent years, Pakistan has insisted that unless progress were made toward solving the Kashmir problem there was little point in trying to improve other aspects of India-Pakistan relations. In keeping with this approach, Islamabad has been unwilling to ease long-standing limitations on trade and other bilateral restrictions unless India agreed to tackle the Kashmir issue. Most of the time, the Indians have called for a general easing of tensions and discussion of all matters, although they have long asserted that the Kashmir issue was solved.

Relations between New Delhi and Islamabad have swung back and forth over the past two decades, perhaps reaching their lowest point in the wake of the Kargil episode. Even when bilateral talks have taken place, these have failed up until now to make significant progress toward reducing tensions and establishing more normal relations. One side or the other has always found a reason not to proceed. Ironically, in April 1948, Muhammad Ali Jinnah in an extended talk with Paul Alling, the first American ambassador to Pakistan, stressed that he wanted U.S.-Canadian relations to serve as a model for Pakistan's ties with India. History regrettably has unfolded in a very different way.

## Afghanistan

After Pakistan became independent, Afghanistan refused to accept the border imposed by the British in the 1890s—called the Durand line after the British negotiator— and angered the Pakistanis by urging the creation of an independent homeland for the Pashtuns from the territory of the NWFP. The Durand line, in fact, left the Pashtun ethnic community on both sides of the border. In Pakistan, Pashtuns comprised the majority of the population in the NWFP and a significant minority in Balochistan. In Afghanistan, Pashtuns were the largest ethnic group. The rulers of Afghanistan for more than a century before the end of the monarchy in 1973 were Pashtuns.

Until 1979, relations fluctuated between periods of calm and tension. Although annoyed by the Afghans, Pakistan regarded the troubles with its weaker and landlocked neighbor as manageable. Even after Afghan Communists seized power in 1978, Pakistan was prepared to work with Kabul (the Afghan capital). However, Islamabad adopted a different attitude toward the Babrak Kamal regime imposed by the Soviet military— the first time Moscow had sent its troops into a country outside the Iron Curtain. Along with the Muslim world, the West and China, Pakistan was shocked by the Soviet intervention and feared that it might be the next target. President Zia ul-Haq publicly opposed the Soviet action, offered haven to Afghan refugees who fled across the porous border, and secretly provided arms for the fledgling anti-Soviet resistance movement. Zia agreed to cooperate in this effort with the Carter Administration. Washington, in turn, agreed that the CIA would funnel help to the Afghan resistance or the mujahideen, as they were called, through Pakistan's ISI. After Ronald Reagan became President in 1981, aid for the mujahideen greatly increased.

With a safe haven in Pakistan and large numbers of the doughty Afghans ready to fight a holy war against the Soviets, the mujahideen, to the surprise of many observers, more than held their own against the Red Army. Without increasing the military commitment beyond roughly 100,000 soldiers, Soviet forces could control the urban areas, but the mujahideen held sway in the countryside. In late 1986, reformist Soviet leadership under Mikhail S. Gorbachev decided to cut its losses and withdraw from Afghanistan, much as the United States had withdrawn from Vietnam a decade before. UN-sponsored negotiations at Geneva, Switzerland, moved into high gear. On April 14, 1988, the Soviet Union, the United States, Pakistan and Afghanistan signed an accord for a phased withdrawal of the Red Army.

It was widely expected that the Afghan Communist regime would crumble after the Soviet forces left and be replaced by the mujahideen. Pakistan had visions of a friendly Afghanistan that would no longer cause trouble and would provide strategic depth against India. However, the Najibullah government stubbornly held its own, remaining in power for over two years after the Soviet military's departure. Only when the Soviet Union itself disintegrated in 1991, did the Communist regime in Kabul collapse. Although the mujahideen were able to establish a government, peace did not follow. Instead, different Afghan factions were soon at each other's throats, with their conflict increasingly a struggle between various ethnic groups. Thus, although the Soviets left Afghanistan, Pakistan enjoyed few fruits of victory. The potentially lucrative trade routes to the newly independent states of Central Asia remained blocked.

After 1991, the Americans, who had continued their support for the mujahideen against the Afghan Communists, departed the scene, leaving Pakistan to deal with its unstable neighbor, the Kalashnikov culture and a serious drug problem. Continued fighting and unrest deterred most Afghan refugees from returning to their homeland.

Pakistan first backed Pashtun mujahideen commander and Islamic hard-liner Gulbuddin Hekmetyar, long a favorite of the ISI. In late 1994, however, Islamabad shifted its support to a new Pashtun group, the Taliban or student movement, that had emerged as a force around the southern Afghan city of Kandahar. Mainly comprising Afghan war veterans, the core of the Taliban were graduates of madrasas that were run by followers of the fundamentalist Deobandi school of Sunni Islam affiliated with a faction of Pakistan's Jamiat-ul-Ulema-e-Islam party.

Over the course of the next two years, with the backing of Pakistan's ISI, the Taliban swept aside other mujahideen groups. In September 1996, it captured Kabul and was recognized diplomatically by Pakistan, Saudi Arabia and the United Arab Emirates—but by no one else. Although the Taliban succeeded in imposing peace, it also imposed its harsh version of Sunni Islam, barring women from schools and work, banning television and Western music, and forcing men to grow beards.

Since then, the Taliban has gained control over almost all of Afghanistan. Only Tajik leader and veteran mujahideen commander Ahmed Shah Masoud continues to hold out in the far northeastern corner of the country and in the Panjshir valley northeast of Kabul. The Taliban's policies toward women, its willingness to harbor Islamic extremists and terrorists like Osama bin Laden, and its support for Islamic extremist movements elsewhere have made the movement an international pariah and the target for sanctions by the UN Security Council. Despite sharp foreign criticism and pressure, Islamabad has continued its support for the Taliban.

## The Muslim World

The stress placed on Islam during the struggle for a Muslim homeland in India ensured that solidarity with other West Asian Muslim countries would stand high on the foreign policy agenda. Pakistan vocally opposed the creation of Israel and staunchly supported the Arab cause in UN deliberations. Relations with other Muslim states, however, were uneven during the 1950s and 1960s. Pakistan's adherence in 1955 to the Baghdad Pact and the Southeast Asia Treaty Organization (SEATO) caused friction with Arab countries such as Egypt and Saudi Arabia, which favored a nonaligned approach. At the same time, close ties developed with pro-Western states, such as Jordan, Turkey and neighboring Iran.

After the loss of East Pakistan moved Pakistan's psychological center of gravity westward toward the Persian Gulf and the Middle East, Zulfikar Ali Bhutto successfully cultivated warm relations with the countries of the region. Following the rise in oil prices after the crisis of 1973, Pakistan benefited from preferential treatment and financial aid from Saudi Arabia and other Persian Gulf producers. In 1974, Bhutto hosted a glittering 38-nation summit of the Organization of the Islamic Conference at Lahore.

Relations with neighboring Iran, with which Pakistan shares an extended if sparsely populated border in arid Balochistan, were generally friendly until differences in recent years over the Taliban in Afghanistan. Despite Pakistan's close ties with the shah, Islamabad accommodated quickly to the Iranian Revolution. During the Afghan war, both Tehran and Islamabad supported the anti-Soviet resistance, although Iran backed Shiite groups and did not coordinate its help with Pakistan. The rise of the stridently anti-Shia Taliban, however, has resulted in bilateral frictions. In 1995, Tehran was upset by the Taliban's capture of Herat in western Afghanistan, an area where Iranian influence has traditionally been strong. Tehran was even angrier in 1998 when the Taliban killed a number of Iranian diplomats during the capture of the northern city of Mazar-i-Sharif. Along with Russia, Iran has become a major source of arms and equipment for Masoud in his ongoing struggle against the Pakistani-backed Taliban. Since the revolution in Iran, Tehran has supported Shiite groups in Pakistan. (Sunni groups were backed initially by Iraq, when it was at war with Iran, and more recently by Saudi Arabia.)

Initially, relations with the then neutralist Persian Gulf state were strained by Pakistan's alliance with the West. Ties improved after Pakistan stationed a substantial military force in Saudi Arabia to provide support for the regime. The Saudis rewarded this and Bhutto's wooing of the Saudi capital, Riyadh, with substantial amounts of financial aid in the 1970s. Relations became especially friendly during the Afghan war in the 1980s when the Saudis matched American financial aid to the mujahideen and welcomed Zia's emphasis on Islam. In recent years, Saudi aid, including petroleum supplies on a concessional basis, has helped prop up the sagging Pakistani economy. The oil-rich Persian Gulf state, home to Islam's holy city of Mecca, has thus become an increasingly important variable in Pakistan's foreign policy calculus. General Musharraf's first foreign trip was to Riyadh, and in December 2000 he felt constrained by Saudi pressure to release Nawaz Sharif from prison and allow him and his family to go into exile in Saudi Arabia.

The emergence of five independent Muslim republics in Central Asia after the collapse of the Soviet Union added a potentially important new dimension to Pakistan's foreign policy. Initially, Islamabad had high hopes for the development of significant trading relationships and close political ties with the new states. Expectations have been frustrated, however, by continued turmoil in Afghanistan that has blocked trade routes between Pakistan and Central Asia. Islamabad's intimate ties with the Taliban have also created bilateral problems with the former Soviet republics, especially as Islamic fundamentalist groups have become the main opposition to the Central Asian regimes.

Chinese Premier Zhu Rongji stands at a welcoming ceremony given him in Islamabad by General Pervez Musharraf (r.), May 11, 2001. China and Pakistan have been de facto allies since the mid-1960s. The link with China has become Pakistan's key security pillar.

## People's Republic of China

Like India, Pakistan recognized the Chinese Communists after they had defeated the Nationalists in 1949. Despite the fact that it joined the anti-Communist SEATO and Baghdad Pact military alliances, the leaders in Karachi strove to maintain civil relations with Beijing. At the 1955 Afro-Asian conference in Bandung, Indonesia, Prime Minister Muhammad Ali Bogra stressed to Chinese Premier Zhou Enlai that his country was not anti-Chinese. In 1956, Prime Minister Hussein Shaheed Suhrawardy exchanged friendly state visits with the Chinese leader. In 1961, Ayub switched Pakistan's vote in the UN General Assembly to support seating the Communists in place of the Nationalists.

The fundamental policy shift occurred after the 1962 Sino-

Indian border conflict. In keeping with the saying that the enemy of my enemy is my friend, Pakistan and China, each of which had profound difficulties with India, found a basis for rapprochement. Even though Presidents Kennedy and Johnson urged Ayub to limit Pakistan's ties with the Chinese, Pakistan's president forged ahead, to Washington's growing annoyance. And after the United States cut off military aid in 1965, China stepped in to become Pakistan's principal source of arms and equipment, and the two countries became de facto allies.

During the Nixon Administration (1969–74), ironically, the White House used Islamabad's friendly relations with Beijing, previously the source of intense U.S.-Pakistan friction, to facilitate the opening to China. The link with China has remained a key security pillar for Pakistan. Beijing has provided large amounts of conventional military equipment and has also assisted Pakistan in developing its nuclear weapons and related missile-delivery capability.

Pakistan's support for the Taliban and other radical Islamic groups with links to fundamentalists in China's Sinkiang province, however, has raised eyebrows in Beijing. The Chinese have toned down their support for Pakistan on Kashmir, for example, refusing to back the rash incursion in Kargil in May 1999. Ties between China and Pakistan, nonetheless, continue to be close. Both Beijing and Islamabad appear to place great value on maintaining a strong bilateral relationship.

## The Soviet Union, then Russia

In contrast to its good relations with China, Pakistan's ties with the Soviet Union and with Russia, its successor state, have been strained. In the early years of independence, Soviet dictator Joseph Stalin regarded Pakistan and India as bourgeois democracies still tied to the apron strings of the British. For its part, Muslim Pakistan looked with distaste on revolutionary and atheistic Soviet communism. Relations turned frosty after Pakistan joined the Western camp in 1954 and became frigid in May 1960 when Moscow shot down an American U-2 spy plane that had taken off from Peshawar on its supposedly secret overflight of the Soviet Union.

Nonetheless, later in the 1960s, relations began to thaw. As Pakistan sought to reduce its foreign policy dependence on the Americans, Ayub Khan became the first Pakistani leader to travel to the Soviet Union. During his 1965 visit, Ayub made progress toward reduced tensions and his second visit to Moscow in 1968 led to a considerable improvement in relations. The Soviets agreed to increase economic assistance and also, to India's great annoyance, to provide Pakistan with military assistance. As a tacit quid pro quo, Ayub decided not to extend the lease on the large U.S. intelligence communications intercept facility located near Peshawar in the NWFP.

After Ayub Khan departed the scene, relations again cooled. In 1969, when Sino-Soviet tensions were at their peak, Pakistan rebuffed pressure from Moscow to distance itself from China. In turn, the Soviets refused to provide additional military equipment to Pakistan and reverted to a more pro-India South Asia policy. During the 1971 East Pakistan crisis, Moscow firmly supported New Delhi and concluded a friendship treaty with India. In the 1980s, Zia ul-Haq's policy toward Afghanistan caused new tensions and saw considerable Soviet pressure on Pakistan. The Red Army's withdrawal from Afghanistan, the end of the cold war and the disintegration of the Soviet Union have not led to a significant improvement in Pakistan's ties to the successor Russian government. The continued flow of arms from Russia to India has upset the Pakistanis; in turn, Islamabad has annoyed Moscow by its efforts to procure military equipment from the Ukraine. An additional source of friction has come from Islamabad's support for the Taliban in Afghanistan and the latter's backing for the rebellion in Chechnya, which is trying to wrest its independence from Russia, as well as for Islamic fundamentalist movements in the newly independent Central Asian Muslim states.

# 6

# The U.S. and Pakistan

W HEN PAKISTAN gained its independence, few observers would have predicted the roller-coaster-like fluctuation in relations with the United States. In August 1947, Washington anticipated friendly relations with Pakistan but perceived few important interests in the new nation. In the fall of 1947, when Pakistan sought a massive $5 billion in economic and military assistance, it received scant satisfaction—the Americans provided a mere $10 million in aid. Despite repeated rebuffs, the Pakistanis persisted in courting the United States in the hope of gaining the support of a major external power to balance India's far greater strength. The Truman Administration wished Pakistan well, but was unwilling to risk trouble with India by establishing a close security relationship.

### 'Most Allied Ally in Asia'

This view changed in 1953 after the Eisenhower Administration took office. Interested in employing Pakistani forces to bolster the defense of the Middle East against the perceived threat from the Soviet Union, the United States signed a military assistance agreement with an eager Pakistan in 1954. The following year, Karachi joined both SEATO and the Baghdad Pact to become what Ayub Khan later called the U.S.'s "most allied ally in Asia." For almost a decade, U.S.-Pakistan relations flourished. Washington became Pakistan's largest source of military and economic aid. In turn, Pakistan allowed the Americans to establish the large intelligence communications facility outside Peshawar and to use the Peshawar airport to fly the supersecret U-2 aircraft over the Soviet Union.

But the national interests and policy aims of the two countries differed in important respects. The United States wanted Pakistan as a partner against the Soviets and the Chinese. Although anti-Communist, Pakistan wanted U.S. help against the threat it perceived from India. Although the United States disliked Indian neutralism, it did not see India as an enemy and tried to maintain good relations with both countries. The Americans were never willing to accede to Pakistan's request for a firm security commitment against an attack by India. The 1959 U.S.-Pakistan bilateral security agreement limited the American commitment to help Pakistan in case of Communist aggression. During the Kennedy and Johnson Administrations, U.S. envoys gave oral commitments of help in the case of an attack by India, but Washington did not put these in writing. The one exception was a secret November 5, 1962, aide-mémoire given Ayub by Ambassador Walter McConaughy. When Ayub asked that the commitment of U.S. help against India be made public, the State Department issued only a watered-down version.

## The Alliance Unravels

This divergence in aims surfaced for all to see in late 1962 when India became involved in a border war with China. After the Kennedy Administration decided to supply military aid to New Delhi, an angry Ayub responded by moving closer to Beijing. His action upset the Americans, who regarded China as their principal foe in Asia. Bilateral relations worsened after President Johnson brusquely withdrew an invitation for Ayub to visit in April 1965. When war broke out between Pakistan and India in September 1965, Johnson not only refused to help, but suspended military and economic aid. Although the United States took similar action with India, Pakistan, which was almost entirely dependent on American assistance, suffered much more. Pakistanis felt betrayed by their supposed ally. After Ayub refused to extend the lease for the intelligence communications facility, the alliance was dead for all practical purposes.

## The Nixon Tilt

This changed, however, after Richard M. Nixon, a longtime friend of Pakistan, became President in 1969. Pakistan's relations with China, its cardinal sin for Kennedy and Johnson, became a cardinal virtue when Nixon privately sought Islamabad's help in opening a new relationship with Beijing. The coincidence of Henry Kissinger's secret trip to China in July 1971—the climax of a two-year covert diplomatic effort—with the East Pakistan crisis suddenly put South Asia at the center of U.S. foreign policy concerns. Regarding Pakistan as an ally and India as a Soviet surrogate, Nixon perceived the crisis as part of the global balance-of-power struggle rather than as another act in the ongoing regional struggle between India and Pakistan. For this reason, and to protect the still-fragile opening to China, the Nixon Administration "tilted" toward Pakistan throughout the crisis.

Close and friendly bilateral relations between Washington and Islamabad continued after the 1971 India-Pakistan war ended. The White House, nonetheless, felt unable to lift the embargo imposed in 1965 on arms transfers to Pakistan until February 1975. Because of its army's harsh suppression of the East Pakistanis during 1971, Pakistan remained in public disfavor in the United States.

The election of Carter as President in 1976 and his emphasis on nuclear nonproliferation, democracy and human rights resulted in a further fluctuation in relations, this time a sharp downturn. The Carter Administration was unhappy about the

Pakistan military's ouster of Zulfikar Ali Bhutto and his subsequent execution. The Americans were also upset by Pakistan's clandestine effort to match the nuclear-explosive capability that India had demonstrated in May 1974. Washington twice suspended aid as a sanction against Pakistan. Relations hit rock bottom on November 21, 1979, when an angry mob sacked the U.S. embassy in Islamabad. Four employees died and 137 others nearly lost their lives after being trapped in the embassy communications vault.

## Afghan War Partnership

Relations dramatically changed once more, just five weeks later, when the Soviet military intervened in Afghanistan. With the Red Army at the Khyber Pass, the traditional invasion gateway to South Asia, Pakistan became a "frontline state." President Carter revived the 1959 U.S. commitment to Pakistan's security against Communist attack and offered to resume military and economic aid. When he proposed a $200 million annual program, President Zia ul-Haq undiplomatically responded, "peanuts." Despite this, Zia agreed to boost covert cooperation in support of the fledgling Afghan resistance movement.

After Ronald Reagan succeeded Carter as President in 1981, the two countries quickly reached agreement on a far larger aid package, one amounting to $600 million a year, and a further expansion of covert cooperation. The Americans also agreed privately that the nuclear issue would not be the centerpiece of relations, but warned the Pakistanis against exploding a nuclear device. Unlike the alliance of the 1950s, the partnership of the 1980s was based on a strong shared opposition to the Soviet presence in Afghanistan. President Zia was warmly received in Washington in 1982. Four years later, in 1986, President Reagan welcomed Prime Minister Muhammad Khan Junejo to the White House as a further sign of cordial U.S.-Pakistan relations.

The nuclear issue, however, kept simmering below the surface. Although President Zia repeatedly assured U.S. visitors that Pakistan did not intend to develop nuclear weapons, intelligence reports told a different story, indicating that the clandestine program was making slow but tangible progress toward its goal. When the "aid for Pakistan" package came up for renewal in 1985, the Reagan Administration had to accept an amendment introduced by Senator Larry Pressler (R-S.D.), cutting off aid if the President concluded Pakistan had developed a nuclear device. At the time, ironically, the Pressler amendment was regarded as a means to continue aid and to fend off stronger legislative restrictions.

As the 1980s drew to a close, the unexpected withdrawal of the Red Army from Afghanistan and the equally unexpected end of the cold war altered the policy dynamic once more. Pakistan's strategic importance to the United States declined and, as the nuclear program continued to progress, pressure to impose sanctions grew. In 1989, President George Bush tried to work out a modus vivendi under which Pakistan would continue to receive U.S. aid as long as it froze its nuclear program. Since Pakistan had reportedly achieved a nuclear capability in 1987 or 1988, the arrangement, in effect, permitted Islamabad to maintain its deterrent against India and to continue to receive more than half a billion dollars in American assistance annually.

## The Pressler Ax Falls

But a year later, in 1990, the U.S. intelligence community reached the firm conclusion that Pakistan had taken the final step toward possessing a nuclear device by machining uranium metal into bomb cores. Washington told Islamabad that it would have to "roll back" this capability by destroying the bomb cores or else face a cutoff of assistance through the imposition of Pressler amendment sanctions. When the Pakistan government—then led by a shaky "troika" of democratically elected Benazir Bhutto, technocrat President Ghulam Ishaq Khan and Army Chief Gen. Mirza Aslam Beg—took no action, a reluctant Bush Administration suspended aid, then running close to $600 million annually, the largest foreign assistance program after Israel and Egypt.

The imposition of Pressler amendment sanctions effectively

ruptured the security relationship between the two countries. Pakistanis bitterly resented the U.S. action. "Now that you no longer need us against the Russians in Afghanistan, we have been discarded like a used Kleenex" was a comment that Americans frequently heard during the 1990s. In Pakistani eyes, the United States had once more proved to be an unreliable friend. Through the decade, relations did not fundamentally improve despite the easing of Pressler amendment sanctions through congressional approval in 1995 of an amendment by Senator Hank Brown (R-Colo.). This removed the bar to economic programs, such as Export-Import Bank lending, and also allowed Pakistan to receive military equipment stranded in the United States when Pressler sanctions were imposed in 1990. The Brown amendment did not, however, permit the transfer of F-16 fighter-bombers that Pakistan owned and had paid for. Indeed, not until December 1998, was the Clinton Administration able to find a way to reimburse the Pakistanis for the F-16s.

Apart from frictions over nuclear policy, narcotics and terrorism problems also bedeviled relations. After drug use and cultivation soared during the Afghan war years, Islamabad pledged close cooperation with U.S.- and UN-sponsored antinarcotics programs. Performance, however, fell so short of promises that for three years, between 1996 and 1998, President Clinton felt obliged to grant a waiver on national-interest grounds in order to avoid the imposition of further sanctions.

Pakistan's close links with Islamic extremist groups, some of which were involved in terrorist acts against the United States, were another source of friction. Islamabad's support for the insurgency in Kashmir and its intimate ties with the Taliban movement in Afghanistan raised the possibility of the U.S. State Department labeling Pakistan as a state that officially sponsored terrorism. In the end, Washington held back from this drastic step but continued to be deeply worried over Pakistani links to fundamentalist groups. Concern on this score increased greatly after Osama bin Laden, a Saudi Arabian Islamic radical, whom the United States blamed for the 1998 terrorist attacks on U.S.

embassies in Kenya and Uganda, found a haven in Taliban-dominated Afghanistan. Washington urged Islamabad, with little result, to pressure its Taliban friends to hand over bin Laden to acceptable judicial authorities.

## Nuclear Tests and Kargil

Although the Clinton Administration hoped for a nuclear rollback in South Asia, it tacitly accepted the existence of "virtual deterrence" between India and Pakistan. But in May 1998 after the Hindu nationalist Bharatiya Janata Party (Indian People's party) took power in India and carried out a series of nuclear tests, Pakistan followed suit two weeks later. In the interim, President Clinton pleaded in vain with Prime Minister Nawaz Sharif not to match India's tests, offering to resume economic and military aid and to deliver the stranded F-16s. The domestic political pressure in Pakistan, however, was strongly in favor of testing, and U.S. credibility in Islamabad was too weak for Sharif to accept Clinton's offer.

As a result, when Pakistan conducted its own nuclear tests, Washington imposed new sanctions as required by law. Worried that the punishment might sink the nearly bankrupt Pakistani economy, the Clinton Administration quickly loosened the strings to permit the IMF to try to negotiate a stabilization program with Islamabad to stave off economic collapse. The United States also began an extended, but largely inconclusive, dialogue with India and Pakistan on nuclear issues. In these talks, Islamabad essentially adopted the position of refusing to agree to American proposals unless India did so first.

In February 1999, the Clinton Administration warmly praised the India-Pakistan summit at Lahore as a major step toward reducing tensions in the region. Washington was thus dismayed by Pakistan's rash sally across the line of control in northern Kashmir near Kargil in May 1999. Fearing this action could lead to wider conflict between two nuclear-armed nations, President Clinton applied much diplomatic muscle to induce Nawaz Sharif to support pulling back the intruders.

Washington had new concerns after the military took power

in October 1999. Although Americans shed few tears for the inept Nawaz Sharif, the Clinton Administration strongly opposed the overthrow of a democratically elected government. Additional legislatively mandated punishments were imposed, but these had little impact since Pakistan was already so subject to wide-ranging nuclear sanctions.

## Clinton Visits Pakistan Briefly

In March 2000, Clinton paid the first visit to Pakistan by an American President since Nixon spent a day there in August 1969. Despite his disapproval of the army coup, Clinton decided that it was important to remain engaged with Pakistan. In a brief five-hour stop, Clinton conferred with General Musharraf and addressed the Pakistani people on television. Substantively, the two leaders—and U.S. and Pakistani policies—differed over three key issues: Pakistan's active support for the Kashmir insurgency, its backing for the Taliban and other Islamic extremists, and its nuclear policies. While the Bush Administration has spoken of Pakistan as a longtime friend of the United States, discussions during a June 2001 visit to Washington by Foreign Minister Abdul Sattar focused on these issues, along with the return of democratic government.

## A DISAPPOINTING HALF CENTURY AND AN UNCERTAIN FUTURE

Over the past half century, Pakistan's achievements have fallen short of the bright hopes of 1947. In 1971, the east wing, unhappy over its treatment by the western-dominated central government, broke away to become an independent country, Bangladesh. In contrast to neighboring India, where the democratic system has become institutionalized, Pakistan has swung back and forth between civilian and military rule and between representative government and dictatorship. No popularly

©Reuters Newmedia Inc./CORBIS

President Bill Clinton at the close of a TV address to the Pakistani nation during his brief visit to Islamabad, March 25, 2000. Earlier in the day, he had urged General Perez Musharraf to seek a peaceful solution in Kashmir and resume dialogue with India.

elected government has ever served out its full term. Political stability has yet to be achieved.

Economically, Pakistan has registered considerable progress in agriculture and industry, but chronic mismanagement, poor policy choices and neglect of education, health and other basic human-development needs have resulted in overall performance below its potential. Defense spending, in particular, has been a constant and heavy drain on the budget, comprising 25 percent to 30 percent of central government outlays and running between 5 percent and 6 percent of GNP.

From its inception, relations with India have dominated Pakistan's foreign and security policies. Pakistan has felt threatened by its larger neighbor, with which it has fought three wars, including the one in 1971 that resulted in independence for East Pakistan. Now that both India and Pakistan possess nuclear weapons, their half-century-old dispute over Kashmir has become a matter of graver international concern.

Over the past five decades, Pakistan's relations with the United States have been extraordinarily volatile. In the 1950s, Pakistan was America's "most allied ally in Asia" and in the 1980s, the indispensable partner in the struggle against the Soviet occupation of Afghanistan. Yet, at other times, serious frictions have marred the relationship even though President Clinton called Pakistan an old friend during his brief visit there in March 2000.

Against the wide swings of the past 54 years, predicting the future of U.S.-Pakistan relations is hazardous. Pakistan's location at the junction of West, South and Central Asia gives it strategic importance. It is a large Muslim state of some 150 million people. The coming to power of a fundamentalist regime would have a profoundly negative impact not only in South and Central Asia, but throughout the Islamic world. Helping to avoid this is clearly an important American interest. Similarly, averting a nuclear holocaust on the subcontinent is a key U.S. policy goal, one that ensures that Washington will remain engaged with Pakistan in the years to come.

Predicting Pakistan's own future is equally hazardous. In the 1960s, and again in the 1980s, the country stood on the edge of middle-income status, but because of poor policy choices and inadequate leadership failed to cross the threshold. Despite present grave problems, the outlook could improve once again if Pakistan were to enjoy a period of political stability, better governance and sounder economic policies, and to focus its attention on tackling domestic shortcomings rather than allowing itself to be obsessed with India. Pakistan is a flawed not a failed state. But if the country does not do better than in the past, its troubles are likely to continue and could even worsen, with serious consequences for the region and the wider world.

# Talking It Over

## *A Note for Students and Discussion Groups*

This issue of the HEADLINE SERIES, like its predecessors, is published for every serious reader, specialized or not, who takes an interest in the subject. Many of our readers will be in classrooms, seminars or community discussion groups. Particularly with them in mind, we present below some discussion questions—suggested as a starting point only—and references for further reading, as well as pertinent online resources.

## Discussion Questions

Throughout its 54 years as an independent nation, Pakistan has alternated between civilian and military rule and been plagued by political instability. The current leader, President Pervez Musharraf, has said that the military will return the country to civilian government by October 2002, three years after the army overthrew Prime Minister Nawaz Sharif. Why has Pakistan been unable to establish a stable political system? What were the major failings of the previous popularly elected governments of Sharif and Benazir Bhutto? How effective has the Musharraf regime been in setting the stage for steadier, more effective democratic governance?

In recent years, Islamic fundamentalist elements have gained strength in the wake of Pakistan's support for jihad or holy war against the Soviet occupation of Afghanistan in the 1980s and against the Indians in Kashmir during the 1990s. What are the prospects for the fundamentalists taking power? Why does the Musharraf regime appear wary of tackling Islamic extremists head-on? What would be the consequences of a fundamentalist-dominated regime for Pakistan, for the region, and for the United States?

Since 1996, the radical Taliban (student) movement has gained control of most of neighboring Afghanistan with the support of Pakistan. Although the Taliban regime has brought peace to the areas under its control, it has become an international pariah because of its treatment of women, imposition of extraordinarily strict Islamic norms, and actions such as destroying the world-famous statues of the Buddha at Bamiyan and providing a haven for Osama bin Laden, who the United States believes organized the August 1998 terrorist attacks on U.S. embassies in Africa. Why does Pakistan continue to back the Taliban? How does this policy affect relations with the United States? What impact does the Taliban have on life in Pakistan?

Pakistan's overriding foreign policy and national security preoccupation has been relations with India, with whom it has fought three wars, two triggered by their long-lasting dispute over Kashmir. Now that both countries have nuclear weapons, their festering differences have become even more dangerous. Why have Pakistan and India been unable to get along? What are the prospects for reduced tensions? for progress toward a settlement of the Kashmir dispute? What role can or should the United States play?

U.S.-Pakistan relations have been like a roller-coaster ride, marked by alliance ties and close partnership during the Eisenhower, Nixon and Reagan Administrations and cool or tense relations when Kennedy, Johnson, Carter and Clinton occupied the White House. In the Afghan war years, only Israel and Egypt received more U.S. aid. But currently Pakistan is under extensive sanctions because of its nuclear weapons and military regime. Why have relations been so volatile? Do you think the two countries should try to stabilize and improve their ties? If so, how? Should the United States lift sanctions against Pakistan?

The Pakistan economy is facing serious difficulties: a major debt burden, sluggish growth, rapidly rising population, low literacy level, heavy defense expenditures, and inadequate tax revenues. What are some of the reasons for the poor economic performance? What are the prospects for improvement? How well has the Musharraf regime done in addressing underlying problems? Apart from possibly lifting sanctions, what other steps can or should the Bush Administration take to help Pakistan?

Overall, Pakistan has had a disappointing first half century, marred by political instability, the growing threat of fundamentalism, inadequate economic growth, continued friction with India and the resultant heavy expenditure on defense, including nuclear weapons. Do you agree that Pakistan remains a flawed but not a failed state? What are the most important steps it can take to avert national failure and to attain a better future for its 150 million people?

## Annotated Reading List

Akhund, Iqbal, *Trial and Error: The Advent and Eclipse of Benazir Bhutto.* Karachi, Oxford University Press, 2000. An insightful account of Benazir Bhutto's first term as prime minister by a retired Pakistani diplomat who served as her national security adviser.

Burki, Shahid Javed, *Pakistan, Fifty Years of Nationhood*, 3rd ed. Boulder, Colo., Westview Press, 1999. The recently published third edition of retired World Bank economist Burki provides a rounded and up-to-date picture of Pakistan's difficult first half century. The best single volume on Pakistan's politics, economics and security policies.

Cohen, Stephen P., *The Pakistan Army*, 2nd ed. New York, Oxford University Press, 1999. Currently at the Brookings Institution, Professor Cohen has brought his valuable study of Pakistan's army up-to-date with an extended introductory essay covering the 1980s and 1990s.

Ganguly, Sumit, *The Crisis in Kashmir: Portents of War, Hopes of Peace*. Cambridge, Mass., Cambridge University Press, 1997. Professor Ganguly, now at the University of Texas, has authored a thoughtful analysis of the past decade of insurgency in Kashmir and outlined possible solutions.

Harrison, Selig S., Kreisberg, Paul H., and Kux, Dennis, eds., *India and Pakistan: The First Fifty Years*. Cambridge, Mass., Cambridge University Press, 1998. A readable account by nine American scholars of Pakistan's (and India's) political, economic, social and foreign policy developments and U.S. dealings with South Asia.

Kux, Dennis, *The United States and Pakistan, 1947–2000: Disenchanted Allies*. Baltimore, Md., Johns Hopkins University Press and Washington, D.C., Woodrow Wilson Center Press, 2001. A comprehensive history of U.S.-Pakistan political and security relations from independence to President Clinton's March 2000 visit.

Noman, Omar, *Pakistan: A Political and Economic History since 1947*. London, Kegan Paul International, 1990. An excellent overall analysis of Pakistan's political and economic development through the Zia years.

Rashid, Ahmed, *Taliban: Militant Islam, Oil and Fundamentalism*. New Haven, Conn., Yale University Press, 2000. The best account of the coming to power of the Taliban in Afghanistan and that regime's links with Pakistan. Written by an experienced Lahore-based Pakistani journalist and Central Asia specialist.

Sattar, Abdul, "Foreign Policy," *Pakistan in Perspective, 1947–1997.* Edited by Rafi Raza. Karachi, Oxford University Press, 1998. A comprehensive account of foreign policy developments as viewed by a senior Pakistani diplomat who is currently serving as his country's foreign minister.

Stern, Jessica, "Pakistan's Jihad Culture." *Foreign Affairs*, Nov./Dec. 2000. A piercing if disturbing analysis of the impact of Islamic fundamentalism on Pakistan.

Talbot, Ian, *Pakistan: A Modern History.* London, Hurst, 1998. A comprehensive account and clear analysis of Pakistan's troubled political life.

Wolpert, Stanley A., *Jinnah of Pakistan: A Life.* New York, Oxford University Press, 1984. A well-written and researched biography of Pakistan's founder by a leading American South Asia specialist.

# Online Resources

**ASIA FOUNDATION,** 465 California St., 14th floor, San Francisco, CA 94104; (415) 982-4640; Fax (415) 392-8863 ▪ The website of this private nonprofit organization provides current news articles and analyses of events in Asian countries to advance mutual interests of the United States and Asia.
**www.asiafoundation.org**

**ASIASOURCE,** 725 Park Ave., New York, NY 10021; (212) 288-6400; Fax (212) 517-8315 ▪ A resource of the Asia Society, this website contains current information on events in Asia, including up-to-date coverage of the Kashmir conflict.
**www.asiasource.org**

**PAKISTAN EMBASSY,** 2315 Massachusetts Ave., NW, Washington, DC 20008; (202) 939-6200; Fax (202) 387-0484 ▪ An official website that includes background information, press releases, government policy and links to government agencies and organizations.
**www.pakistan-embassy.com**

**PAKISTAN VIRTUAL LIBRARY** ▪ This site contains a wealth of articles on the history of Pakistan, as well as information on current conditions and policies.
**www.clas.ufl.edu/users/gthursby/pak**

For more information, visit FPA's online Resource Library at **www.fpa.org**, and search using "Pakistan" as your key word. You will find dozens of documents, organization links, maps, news sources, reports, book descriptions, and other tools to assist you with your research.

# Editorial Advisory Committee

# FPA.org

## GREAT DECISIONS ONLINE

Download the latest GD Updates, join a discussion group, access resources for using Great Decisions, find out about Great Decisions Television in your area or read the latest National Opinion Ballot Report.

## GLOBAL FORUMS

Guides bring you nonpartisan analysis, links, the most up-to-the-minute information and online discussion on current global concerns.

## FPA BOOKSTORE

You can order our HEADLINE SERIES, *Great Decisions,* Special Publications and the best of global affairs publishing in Editor's Picks in our secure, online bookstore.

## JOB BOARD

Jobs and internships in global affairs organizations, including international nonprofits and government agencies.

## THE RESOURCE LIBRARY

Research, analysis, news, maps and organizations searchable by issue and region.

## E-NEWSLETTERS

The latest in foreign policy sent to your In Box. Sign up for one of our free weekly newsletters today.

## EVENTS

Global affairs events sponsored by FPA, the World Affairs Councils of America, international organizations and universities.

### Connect to a community of global thinkers
### Visit FPA.org today

# HEADLINE SERIES, published since 1935, provides
readers with concise, timely analysis of a specific area or issue in
world affairs. These informative pocket-sized books are written
by foreign policy experts, journalists and other authorities.

—◦—

## AVAILABLE ISSUES OF CONTINUING INTEREST

### Global Concerns

## Geographic Areas

## U.S. Foreign Policy

## SUBSCRIPTION RATES

$20.00 for 4 issues; $35.00 for 8 issues; $50.00 for 12 issues.

Single copy price $5.95; double issue $11.25; special issue $10.95.

Discount 25% on 10 to 99 copies; 30% on 100 to 499; 35% on 500 and over.

**Write or call for a free catalog.**

# Forthcoming HEADLINE SERIES

## Mexico: Changing of the Guard
By GEORGE W. GRAYSON

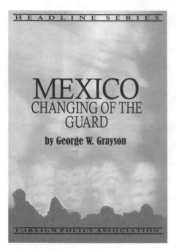

HEADLINE SERIES 323
Fall 2001
ISBN # 0-87124-199-4
Product ID # 31510
Price: $5.95

VICENTE FOX QUESADA of the center-right National Action party (PAN) became president of Mexico on December 1, 2000, with ambitious goals for domestic and foreign policy. Yet the populist leader, formerly a business executive at Coca-Cola, faces opposition both within his party and from outside, with an array of potent foes trying to stymie his plans. This HEADLINE SERIES looks at the initiatives Fox has tackled so far, including defusing the Chiapas conflict, economic reform and relations with the United States, European countries and other nations in the Western Hemisphere. Evaluating the successes and failures of the past seven months, Grayson provides an analysis and forecast of Fox's ability to transform Mexico into a truly modern, democratic, humanitarian country.

GEORGE W. GRAYSON teaches government at the College of William & Mary and has written 12 books and monographs on Mexico, including *A Guide to the 2000 Mexican Presidential Election*, published by the Center for Strategic & International Studies (CSIS), where he is an adjunct fellow.

# FOREIGN POLICY ASSOCIATION

470 Park Avenue South, 2nd Floor ■ New York, NY 10016-6819
Order Toll-Free (800) 477-5836 ■ Fax (212) 481-9275 ■ www.fpa.org

**Sold to:** (please print)

Name _____

School /Address _____

City _____ State _____ Zip _____

Daytime Phone _____

**Ship to:** (please print)

Name _____

School /Address _____

City _____ State _____ Zip _____

Daytime Phone _____

→ Prepayment must accompany all orders from individuals, and must include shipping and handling charges. Libraries, universities and schools using purchase orders may be billed. Orders placed for new accounts are subject to credit approval.

→ New York State residents please add 8.25% sales tax; Canadian residents please add 7% GST.

→ All orders outside the U.S. and its possessions must be prepaid in U.S. funds with a check drawn on a U.S. correspondent bank. Please include shipping and handling charges as noted below.

| PUBLICATION | QTY. | UNIT PRICE | TOTAL |
|---|---|---|---|
|  |  |  |  |
|  |  |  |  |
|  |  |  |  |

| SHIPPING AND HANDLING | | |
|---|---|---|
| **Great Decisions** <br> **Domestic:** Included in price of book <br> **Foreign (including Canada):** <br> $4.00 first copy; <br> $1.00 each additional copy. <br> **Headline Series** <br> $2.50 first copy; <br> $.50 each additional copy. | **SUBTOTAL** |  |
|  | NYS and Canadian residents add sales tax |  |
|  | ← Shipping and handling |  |
|  | **TOTAL** | $ |

## METHOD OF PAYMENT:

❏ Check enclosed (payable to Foreign Policy Association)

❏ PO attached    ❏ American Express    ❏ Visa    ❏ Mastercard

Credit Card # _____

Expiration Date _____ Signature _____